The Hermit of Gully Lake

The Life and Times of Willard Kitchener MacDonald

Joan Baxter

Pottersfield Press, Lawrencetown Beach, Nova Scotia, Canada

Copyright © Joan Baxter 2005

All rights reserved. No part of this publication may be reproduced or used or transmitted in any form or by any means – graphic, electronic or mechanical, including photocopying – or by any information storage or retrieval system, without the prior, written permission of the publisher. Any requests for photocopying, recording, taping or information storage and retrieval systems of any part of this book shall be directed in writing to Access Copyright, The Canadian Copyright Licensing Agency, 1 Yonge Street, Suite 1900, Toronto, Ontario M5E 1E5. This also applies to classroom use.

Library and Archives Canada Cataloguing in Publication

Baxter, Joan

The hermit of Gully Lake : the life and times of Willard Kitchener MacDonald / Joan Baxter.

ISBN 1-895900-70-0

1. MacDonald, Willard Kitchener, 1916-2003. 2. Recluses--Nova Scotia--Biography. 3. Nova Scotia--Biography. I. Title.

FC2345.G84Z49 2005   971.6'04'092   C2005-900552-1

Front cover photo: Shirley Sutherland Miller
Author photo: Karlheinz Eyrich
Cover design: Dalhousie Graphics

Pottersfield Press acknowledges the support of The Canada Council for the Arts, as well as the Nova Scotia Department of Tourism, Culture and Heritage, Cultural Affairs Division. We also acknowledge the financial support of the Government of Canada through the Book Publishing Industry Development Program for our publishing activities.

Pottersfield Press
83 Leslie Road
East Lawrencetown
Nova Scotia, Canada, B2Z 1P8
Website: www.pottersfieldpress.com
To order, phone 1-800-NIMBUS9 (1-800-646-2879)
Printed in Canada

 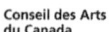 

Contents

Author's note		7
Chapter 1	Laying the legend to rest	12
Chapter 2	The puzzle of the early years	19
Chapter 3	A man with no ties	31
Chapter 4	Troop train jumper	36
Chapter 5	A troubled family	42
Chapter 6	Speak but little, trust but few...	52
Chapter 7	A hermit's home	59
Chapter 8	Snow baths and sun worship	73
Chapter 9	Fiddler in the woods	83
Chapter 10	Proud, stubborn and... healthy	91
Chapter 11	Many helping hands and many visitors	102
Chapter 12	The spiritual dimension	111
Chapter 13	A new hermitage	116
Chapter 14	Lost... then found	125
Chapter 15	Taking care of hermit business	139
Epilogue	The legacy of a legend	143
Acknowledgements		151
Maps		155
Bibliography		158

Dedicated to the memory of Shirley Sutherland Miller
who passed away too soon to see this book in print

Willard Kitchener MacDonald. (Photo by Dr. Gerry Farrell)

Hermit: 1 A person (esp. a man) who from religious motives has retired into solitary life; *esp.* an early Christian recluse. b A person who falsely claims to be a recluse; a beggar. 2 A member of any of various monastic orders. 3 A person who lives in solitude or shuns human society from any motive. *The New Oxford Shorter English Dictionary*, 1995.

Men frequently say to me, "I think you would feel lonesome down there, and want to be nearer folks, rainy and snowy days and nights especially." I am tempted to reply to such – This whole earth which we inhabit is but a point in space. How far apart, think you, dwell the two most distant inhabitants of yonder star, the breadth of whose disc cannot be appreciated by our instruments? Why should I feel lonely? Is not our planet in the Milky Way? This which you put seems to me not to be the most important question. What sort of space is that which separates a man from his fellows and makes him solitary? – Henry David Thoreau, *Walden*

Author's note

Right at the outset, I need to say that much to my regret I never met Willard Kitchener MacDonald, the man known far and wide as the "Hermit of Gully Lake."

It wasn't until the evening of December 3, 2003, that I even heard of this remarkable and enigmatic man who had jumped from a troop train to avoid going off to battle in World War II and lived for more than half a century in the woods around Earltown in northern Nova Scotia. By then, it was already too late to make his acquaintance; he had disappeared and would never again be seen alive. The heavy rains we'd had all day in the area had turned into heavy snowfall, and my two teenagers returned from a day at school in Truro, animated and eager to describe what they had just witnessed as they passed through the community of Earltown. "Downtown Earltown," as it's affectionately called, is not exactly a big or bustling place. Even if you have slowed down in deference to the sixty-kilometre speed limit, you can drive right through it in twenty-nine seconds. There is the landmark General Store and gas pump owned and run by Murphy Stonehouse, a community hall, the Community Church, a cemetery, a Presbyterian church, and there are also a few cozy homes and barns nestled in a quiet rural settling.

But on that day, the quiet had been shattered in Earltown. My children told me there were Search and Rescue helicopters and RCMP vehicles all over the place, and a massive hunt was on for an old man who for decades had lived alone in the woods like a hermit. I was instantly hooked. I collected all the reports about him I could find in the newspapers. I raised the subject of the recluse in every casual conversation I had with people in the area. My curiosity simmered away. I was desperate to find out more. My family will confirm that I drove people crazy.

Unlike just about everyone else in northern Nova Scotia and indeed throughout the province, I had never heard the incredible tale of "The Hermit" before. We had just moved back to Canada after twenty-two years of living in Africa, where my children had spent their childhoods and early teenage years.

I was finding the adjustment to life at the end of a back road in rural Nova Scotia a little, well, challenging. To make matters worse, the weather in our first year back in the country had been pretty wild, even by Nova Scotian standards. The province had just undergone a hurricane that in our area had knocked out power for a week at the end of September and into early October. Early winter snowstorms had already caused more havoc by bringing down still more trees that in turn brought down our power line a second time in just two months. We should have been used to living without electric power; we had often managed without it in Africa. But it had been different there; it was always warm in West Africa and there was no snow to keep us housebound while awaiting the snowplow.

I was struggling to finish a new book about Africa, but having difficulty summoning the images and stories of that sunny continent from my isolation in northern Nova Scotia, while the days grew shorter and the skies more sombre with winter setting in. In Africa, privacy and solitude had seemed like unattainable luxuries. Now, back in Canada, I had far too much privacy and I rattled around in the huge vacuum left by the move away from Africa. In that first year, I felt a terrible sense of loss – having left a job reporting in wonderful, chaotic, hot and sometimes even dangerous places in West Africa, which from rural Nova Scotia just seemed too far away to be real. I had been away from Canada for too long and no longer felt I fit in anywhere in what was my home and native land. I was a stranger, a social misfit, lonely and on bad days, downright misanthropic. I worried I was becoming or had already become – no other word for it – a hermit.

But of course I wasn't, certainly not in the true sense that Willard Kitchener MacDonald was, "a person who lives in solitude and shuns human society." My dislocation in the new surroundings was just a temporary condition, a simple period of physical and psychological adjustment that everyone makes after a move from one place to another. It usually takes about a year to settle in, stock a house with all the appliances and books and clutter of personal belongings we seem to need around us, to figure out how things work and to find the friends that make a new city or town or even a village feel like "home."

I was no hermit; I was just feeling sorry for myself.

But Willard Kitchener MacDonald was. And the nagging question of what kind of life he led during those sixty years in the woods – without family and the bustle of other people around him, without any comforts or amenities – just wouldn't go away and leave me be.

How on earth had he done it: survive in a dingy hovel in the woods in a northern and notoriously cold country on his own through those long winters, buried in snow and silence? How did someone survive the mosquitoes, black flies, deer flies and horseflies of a summer in the Nova Scotian woods? How did someone survive the loneliness and solitude? And more to the point, why would someone choose such hardship and isolation?

My search for his story began in August 2004 with a hike to Gully Lake, to the site of his burned-out hut. The mosquitoes were atrocious, eating me alive. The lake itself was little more than a swamp in the dry heat of summer. And the place felt very, very lonely.

As the Nova Scotia government mused over the decision of whether to turn Gully Lake into a protected wilderness area, I mused about writing a book that would, at least, commemorate – and perhaps offer some insight into – the life and times of Willard Kitchener

MacDonald, who had lived there for so many years, a kind of guardian of Gully Lake.

I underestimated just how difficult it was going to be to delve into the past of this man, trace his family's movements in his early years and his own during and after the war. It meant many, many days on the road, tracking down and visiting with a long list of kind and generous people who willingly shared with me their memories of and reflections on the man. Using the stories they told me, their photographs, their audiotapes and video cassettes, I have managed to reconstruct the bare bones of the "hermit's" story from the many people who did know him – for most of his life, for a few decades and even from just a few visits.

There were also a very few who declined invitations to share their reminiscences for a book. I deeply regret their absence on these pages but accept that not everything can or even should be written down when it comes to the private lives of citizens who did not seek to be "famous." I respect their decision to remain quiet about a man who sought solitude and not the headlines he made.

The making of the man and his story was in an earlier era and in rural communities riddled with secrets, where people rallied around their own with a protective, respectful seal of silence. Even his closest friends do not claim to understand Willard Kitchener MacDonald. Ruth Smith, one of the very few who can say he was her friend, told me, "If there's one thing I wish he had willed to me that would be the knowledge that was in his head."

So, obviously, this book doesn't pretend to unravel much of the deep mystery of what went on in his mind for all those years, what drove him to take the leaps he took – first from a troop train to avoid going to war in Europe and then into the woods to live on his own, long after the Canadian government declared amnesty to deserters in 1950.

Ruth Smith said that one of the sayings that Willard passed on to her children was one that guided him throughout his life: "Speak but little, trust but few." It's a very apt motto for a man who chose to live like a hermit, but it's a bit of an anathema for any writer wishing to get at and tell his story.

In later years, as his legend spread, he became known throughout Nova Scotia and beyond as a tall, elderly, haggard, bearded man with matted hair and soot-covered hands and face, in leaky boots, and his trousers often held up by twine and with broken zippers, who stood with quiet dignity before the cameras as the "Hermit of Gully Lake."

Some of his oldest friends, especially those who knew him when he was young and before the hermit legend spread, knew him only as Willard. They flinch when they hear him referred to as "The Hermit" or even Kitchener. Yet those who knew him in the last three decades of his life, those who befriended him in his tiny hut in Gully Lake, knew him as Kitchener because this is what he told them he wished to be called. He said he wanted to avoid confusion with another Willard MacDonald from Pictou whose mail he claimed he had been receiving.

Given that I never met him, I feel unqualified to use the familiar "Willard," which is what only his oldest friends called him. For that reason I refer to him throughout this book as Kitchener.

"He was his own man," is the phrase nearly all those who knew him fall back on, when searching for a few words to capture his character. He was his own man, but what man was that? That is the question I asked of dozens of people who knew him and the many answers they offered fill the pages of this book.

Chapter 1
Laying the legend to rest

> I had more visitors when I lived in the woods than at any other period in my life; I mean that I had some.
> – Henry David Thoreau, *Walden*.

On July 8, 2004, three men set out from the Community Church in Earltown, Nova Scotia. They hiked up the back trails leading to Gully Lake, a shallow and secluded little body of water surrounded by rolling forested hills in the chain of the Cobequid Mountains that runs across northern Nova Scotia. The men had with them a royal blue velvet bag that held an urn. Inside it were the ashes of Willard Kitchener MacDonald, a man who had spent most of his long life hiding from the outside world in the seclusion of these woodlands, a man the wider world had come to know – usually affectionately and respectfully, occasionally disparagingly and sometimes almost reverentially – as "The Hermit of Gully Lake."

One of the men entrusted with the ashes was Leroy Marshall, Kitchener's unacknowledged son. Leroy had seen and spoken with his father many times over the years, but not once in all Leroy's sixty-four years had Kitchener ever admitted to him that he was his father. Also along on this trek up the hills on that warm day in July was a local farmer who had often visited with Kitchener in his Gully Lake home and chopped firewood for him. The third man was David Smith, from the tiny farming community of Loganville on the north side of the lake.

David had known Kitchener his entire life. His mother Ruth still recalls in vivid detail and with a mischievous smile the raucous, music-filled night that she brought her three-day-old son David home from the hospital. She sat at the pump organ playing along to old-time fiddle tunes with Kitchener and other local music-makers, well past midnight. Ruth says it was at about three in the morning that Kitchener's mother Jessie arrived, saying, "Lord, you fellas get out of here. That woman just got home from the hospital."

Now, forty-five years later, David Smith was making his way up the hill on a sunny, glorious summer day, carrying the remains of his old friend. He and his two companions moved along back paths strewn with massive trees laid flat by Hurricane Juan the previous September. They were headed to the site of Kitchener's former hut set back a few hundred metres from Gully Lake, a remote little spot in a remote little part of Canada's second smallest province. In these hills, Willard Kitchener MacDonald had spent more than half a century surviving what were to most people almost unimaginable physical hardship and inconceivable social seclusion.

Just over a year earlier, Kitchener had suffered a terrible loss when his hut burned down, something many were surprised had not happened years earlier, given the various makeshift items he had used as stoves over the years. The fire was the greatest tragedy in Willard's later life.

Just about all his belongings were lost – his huge collection of dog-eared books, his homemade guitar, the army issue .303 rifle that he probably took with him when he deserted, the snowshoes and wind chimes friends had given him, his long-stemmed "peace pipe," a hubcap he used as a plate and a saucepan, and all his own writings, which he always claimed would one day become a book. But worse than that, he lost the little hut – just six by eight feet according to friends who took the time to measure it – which he had cobbled together from wood and plastic and tin sheets over the years. With it he also lost the secluded refuge that had been his home for decades.

Friends say that after the fire, he was never quite the same. He reluctantly moved into a one-and-a-half storey winterized cabin about a half a kilometre in from the unpaved Kemptown Road, which Colchester County had built for him using his accumulated old age pension funds. That was a home Kitchener had tried out and then quickly abandoned five years earlier, saying it was too noisy with too much traffic on that back road.

Long-time friend Hector MacKenzie laughs at that, remembering that on the day he spent with Kitchener in that government-approved cabin replete with bed, well with pump and privy, "at least two cars passed on the Kemptown Road." But for Kitchener, even two cars were too many. He had lived too long with the sounds of the forest and the animals around him at Gully Lake to adapt now to the noise of the modern world, to which most of us are almost deaf.

Even when he had lived deep in the woods at Gully Lake, he complained to friends that the noise from the pulp mill on Abercrombie Point in Pictou County disturbed his sleep. That pulp mill may indeed spread its noxious stench far and wide in northern Nova Scotia. But it must have taken a very refined pair of ears way over in north Colchester County to even detect, let alone be bothered by, the *noise* the mill makes – about thirty-five kilometres away as the crow flies.

Kitchener had just that very refined set of ears. Occasionally in later years, his friends would take in nurses and doctors to visit him, and some of these were even successful in convincing him to allow them to perform a few basic medical tests. According to one doctor, at the age of almost eighty, Kitchener had the hearing of a healthy sixteen-year-old youth.

David Smith and some of his friends find Kitchener's death in 2003 (or if they are right about when he died, in 2004) particularly tragic. They believe Kitchener might still be alive and well, had well-intentioned friends not summoned medical help when they found him ailing. David thinks his fear of being forced into a hospital or a

Gully Lake, a view of the "end of the road" where Kitchener's remains were found in June 2004; his former hut stood just off to the left, with a view of this end of the lake. (Photo by Joan Baxter)

seniors' home is what drove him to leave the warmth and safety of his new cabin – and to his death.

He died at the very edge of the lake that had become synonymous with his name and legend, just a stone's throw from the site of his burned-out hut. There, where his hut had stood, David and Leroy spread his remains – ashes to ashes. They sprinkled them over the vegetation that had grown up just in front of the former hut and the window Kitchener had used as a door, where he had spent so many hours of his life, strumming his homemade guitar, composing music, reading, and contemplating the beauty around him.

Asked once by a busy young urbanite from Halifax what he did with all his "spare time," Kitchener replied, "I set and think and wonder. Doesn't everyone?"

As they broadcast his ashes that day, Leroy and David reflected on the hardship of Kitchener's life, about the reasons he chose to live as a hermit, and on the tragedy of the fire. The site was still littered with the detritus of his private life: the woodstove that once sat in the middle of his hut; disintegrating pages from *The Chronicle Herald* and assorted books that had not completely burned, including one by Northrop Frye; bits of old bicycle chains and saw blades; dozens and dozens of plastic bottles; and plastic bags filled with old shirts, hats and trousers. A leather mitten with holes had been stuck onto a tree branch and hung there like a last salute.

Although David had heard rumours that the County was going to put up a headstone or plaque to mark the site as the home of the Hermit of Gully Lake, he decided to create a small tribute to his old friend that day. He and Leroy hoisted the rusted little woodstove onto a pair of old skis they found lying in the bushes, and then propped up two ski poles over the stove to form a cross, next to another one they made by lashing together two sticks. As a last touch, they then placed a mouldy hard-cover copy of Farley Mowat's book *Virunga: The Story of Dian Fossey and the Mountain Gorillas of Africa* on top of the stove, and headed back down the trails to Earltown.

Leaving Willard Kitchener MacDonald at peace beside Gully Lake.

It was a fittingly private and quiet end for the Hermit of Gully Lake, despite the fact that in the last decade of his life he had become so widely known that his existence was hardly that of a hermit any more; he had a lot of human company that he did not shun. However, right to the end his did remain a life without any of the amenities that had become the norm – at least in the wealthy world – during his lifetime.

Dozens of people had befriended him since the 1970s, when snowmobiles became common and allowed people from all over the Maritimes to get in to Gully Lake to visit with him in even the worst winter weather. And in recent years, it seems that hardly a weekend went by that small groups of friends, often bringing others with them, didn't make their way up to Kitchener's home in the hills to talk, picnic, bring him a gift bottle or package of tobacco or cigars, a bag of potatoes or rice, or whatever he seemed to need or like, to listen to his stories, jokes and tall tales, and mostly, to make music with him.

People throughout Colchester and Pictou Counties had known MacDonald, or known of him, for decades. Many had gone to great lengths to ensure that he never went hungry. Murphy Stonehouse, who owns and runs the General Store in Earltown, was one of Kitchener's greatest friends and defenders. He seemed to be leery of all the media attention and curious newcomers heading into the hills to try to catch a glimpse of his friend: the increasingly famous "Hermit."

The media had "discovered" Willard Kitchener MacDonald in the 1980s. In February 1986, Lloyd Bogle took the CBC's Wendy Mesley and a television crew into the woods to produce a short item about him for the evening news program in Halifax. In July that year, another CBC journalist produced a report in which she delved into all sorts of personal issues that intrigued people "on the outside," asking Kitchener about his bathing habits and whether he ever used shampoo.

"Not much shampoo around here," he replied quietly.

Sometimes the media reports made his old friends in the community, many of whom had been doing their utmost to protect his privacy and dignity over the years, uncomfortable or even deeply annoyed. One can only guess how Kitchener felt about all the cameras, tape recorders and microphones. In some of the television reports, his body language suggests to me that he felt the intrusion deeply. He often turns away from the camera, lifts his arms to cover his head with his elbows, much like an embattled and overwhelmed boxer might do in the ring against a more powerful opponent.

And yet he could have simply refused to be interviewed or filmed – or even found. So some people believe he loved the attention and that he chose to use the name "Kitchener" almost as if it were a stage name for the new character – the mysterious hermit, a man with no past – that the media and new friends were getting to know, or even create.

As much as he liked to be alone, liked his privacy, he also liked a little drink or two, an afternoon jam session with fiddles and guitars, and in later years he certainly seemed to like the company of those who came to spend time and play music with him.

"He liked to see us come," says Hector MacKenzie, who first got to know Kitchener back in the 1930s and then visited him regularly in the past three decades. "But he also liked to see us go."

So what did drive Willard Kitchener MacDonald into the wilderness? Was it really, as legend has it, that he fled into the woods after jumping a troop train and then stayed there, fearful of capture for the rest of his life, until it grew to include fear of large groups of people, the modern world, and an undying mistrust of the authorities and the wider world in general? Would he have chosen this life of solitude because there was something in his nature that precluded a "normal" life in the rapidly changing post-war times, even if he had not deserted? Was he telling the truth when he told people he wouldn't wish his life on anyone, or merely teasing them, playing with words, telling them what they wanted to hear?

Only he could have answered those questions and, alas, he never would. When his friends posed intimate questions, he offered contradictory answers. He was full of mischief, brimming with ideas and curiosity, deeply musical and spiritual, and most of all he was very private.

This helps explain why he did become a legend in his own time, an enigmatic man who needed so little of what the modern world offered, and who rebuffed any attempts to solve the mystery he and his past presented – a man who will long be remembered simply as the Hermit of Gully Lake.

Chapter 2
The puzzle of the early years

According to his birth certificate, he was born Willard Kitchener MacDonald, in the town of Somerville, Massachusetts, on August 13, 1916. It seems that several people over the years have written to Massachusetts to obtain copies of that birth certificate. Lloyd Bogle in Stewiacke keeps one in a kitchen drawer full of Kitchener memorabilia. He got it by sending away to the U.S.A. in 1971, the year he first met Kitchener. Jarvis and Lillie Stewart in Truro can still produce an original birth certificate for him, issued on July 25, 1986. They obtained it by collecting some basic facts about Kitchener from a relative and sending that away, along with two dollars, to Massachusetts. They hoped that it would help them secure the old age pension for their friend at Gully Lake.

Kitchener, however, never liked to speak about his age, just as he didn't like to speak about his family or his past. As a result, very little is known about his very early years in the United States, or even how his parents, Findlay Howard MacDonald and Jessie E. Sutherland, both from northern Nova Scotia, found themselves there at all, let alone there together with a newborn baby.

The only living person who can shed a little light on this period is Kitchener MacDonald's aunt, Jessie's sister. Born in 1902, the aunt is living today in Moncton, New Brunswick, but is too frail to receive any visitors outside immediate family. Her niece, Kitchener's first cousin, Shirley Sutherland Miller, has visited her aunt regularly and recorded a few of her earliest memories. Some offer glimpses into Jessie's family when she was still a young and eligible woman living with her family on Arthur Street in Truro and Howard MacDonald was a regular visitor to the house.

It was around this time, just before the start of World War I, that Kitchener's maternal grandfather, William Sutherland, won a prize for his work as a salesman for Singer sewing machines. That prize was a large portrait of Lord Horatio Herbert Kitchener, the British military figure who became a colonial war hero for his exploits in recapturing Sudan for the British in 1898 and ending the Boer War in South Africa. Lord Kitchener would later become Britain's war secretary during the Great War of 1914-18. He would not survive the war. On June 6, 1916, he perished in a naval battle in the North Sea.

Hannah Sutherland, Kitchener's maternal grandmother, hung the portrait of Lord Kitchener on the wall of their living room in her Truro home, probably around the time he was named war secretary. It must have left its mark on young Jessie because she would eventually borrow the name for her firstborn son, born in the United States just two months after Lord Kitchener died. The irony of his sharing the name of a British and colonial war hero would not become apparent for many years, not until he jumped from a troop train to avoid going off to World War II in the 1940s.

Kitchener's aunt in Moncton also has memories of listening to Howard MacDonald playing his violin on the front porch of the Sutherland home, particularly Dvorjak's haunting melody "Humouresque."

It may have been that Howard's seductive music and frequent presence around the Sutherland house in Truro were starting to worry Jessie's parents, that they didn't necessarily approve of the young suitor or didn't want things moving along too quickly. Or they may just have decided their daughter would benefit from a visit with relatives in Massachusetts. For whatever reason, one year Jessie did go down to stay with those family relations in the United States, perhaps with Jessie's uncle Alexander. And whether Jessie's parents knew he was planning to or not, whether they approved or not, Howard MacDonald wound up in the U.S. as well.

Howard's father came from the village of Durham, near Pictou, and his mother, Kitchener's grandmother, was born Gunn and raised on Dalhousie Mountain, just east of Gully Lake. This family history comes from Lloyd MacIntosh, who was born the same year as Kitchener and became one of his most trusted friends till his death.

Melvin MacKay, who grew up in East Earltown and knew the MacDonald family when he and Kitchener were young men working together in the area, recalls Howard as a man not easily tied down by regular jobs. "Howard wasn't much of a worker. [He was] all over the country – here, there and everywhere," Melvin says. "He was a great violin player, though, and so was Willard."

Ruth Smith got to know Kitchener and his parents in the mid-1930s, when the MacDonalds moved for a time into a house near her family's farm in Loganville. Kitchener's family lived in what Ruth calls the "Gunn House" that belonged to Howard's uncle, on a backwoods track known as Gunshot Road. Ruth's mother was a close friend to Howard and Jessie, and she recalls that Howard MacDonald was well known for his violin playing in Pictou County and had earned the name "Fiddle Foot." Howard had been trained in classical violin, and some believe he may even have played at Carnegie Hall with symphony orchestras. He liked to liven up his performance by playing the instrument behind his back, and doing all sorts of tricks with the bow.

When Howard went to the United States, he had great ambitions of making it as a violinist in the Vaudeville theatres in Boston, but, according to Ruth Smith, he didn't realize his ambitions because he wasn't able to pick up the music fast enough.

Even if he wasn't successful in his pursuit of a musical career in Vaudeville, Howard's time in the U.S. was not wasted. It produced one very tangible result – a firstborn son. Kitchener's birth certificate gives his father's profession as "mechanic" and his mother's as "housewife" and the couple's address as 7 Heath Street in Somerville. The birth certificate does not give their dates of birth, but according to the family headstone in Durham Cemetery in Pictou County, Howard was born in 1885 and Jessie in 1893, making Kitchener's father thirty-one and his mother twenty-three when he was born.

Kitchener was not the only legacy of Howard and Jessie's time in the United States. Family members recall that they came home not just with a son but also with a new faith. Many who knew the family say they believed the MacDonalds had become adherents of Christian Science. But it is more likely that they subscribed to another of the Christian faiths known as "New Thought" religions that sprang up in the U.S. in the late 1800s, of which Christian Science was perhaps just the best known.

Based on the religious magazines that Jessie gave out to family and friends, it seems the faith they adopted in the United States was called the Unity School of Christianity or simply "Unity." According to its website today, Unity was founded in 1889 in Kansas City, Missouri, by Charles and Myrtle Fillmore. It describes itself as a "worldwide movement of prayer, publishing and education" from its headquarters of Unity Village, near Kansas City, with a "Mediterranean-style campus" that includes "1,400 acres of beautiful countryside including formal gardens, an extensive metaphysical library, bookstore, and the Unity Village Chapel. The peaceful atmosphere and natural beauty attracts spiritual seekers of all faiths and backgrounds."

According to a religious tolerance website that describes the Unity religious movement in Canada, it is a liberal faith that rejects the notions of original sin, the idea that "God is a [sic] elderly superhuman male with a flowing white beard . . . [who is] to be feared," and that Jesus Christ is a deity who asked to be worshipped. Rather, those within the Unity movement follow "a form of pantheism," which sees God existing in all things – human beings, plants, animals, the earth itself. Followers of the faith look on "Jesus as a great healer, miracle worker and mystic" with "direct access to God." They also regard the Genesis story as "an allegory." In short, Unity adherents value the "inspiration and progress made by all the great religions of the world especially Christianity from which they derive the bulk of their beliefs."

The same website says that in the early years, followers of the Unity Church in Canada corresponded directly with the American headquarters at Unity Village in Missouri. During the late 1920s and '30s the Unity Church in Canada went through a "settling out process," which was interrupted by the rise of strong anti-Americanism that developed in Canada following the Depression and by the development of the United Church of Canada as an "ecumenical, cooperative, Christian spiritual experience."

For many years, indeed right up to the 1970s, Jessie gave subscriptions of Unity's religious magazine for children, *Wee Wisdom*, to her nieces and nephews and to friends' children, and subscriptions of the adult publication, *Unity – A Way of Life*, to her adult relatives and friends. Jessie's devotion to this new and unknown doctrine from the United States seems to have caused a certain amount of whispered consternation among her sisters and brothers. There are also reports of tension between Jessie and her sister-in-law, Etta Silver (*née* MacDonald).

It is not clear where the MacDonalds lived on their return to Canada, whether they lived in Pictou and Colchester Counties or if they just moved around from one place to another throughout the two counties or even all around the Maritimes. Some remaining relatives have clear memories of the family moving about from shack to shack, from Dieppe in New Brunswick to the Tantramar Marshes near Amherst, Nova Scotia, and believe their nomadic lifestyle had to do with their missionary activities – that they were trying to "bring people to God."

It seems likely that it was shortly after their return to Canada that Jessie gave birth to a daughter, Kathleen. An undated photograph of Kathleen as a toddler and Kitchener as a very small boy suggests that his sister might have been three or four years his junior.

Their movements in the 1920s and even early 1930s may never be known, but there is some evidence that they struggled financially. Kitchener's first cousin, Shirley Sutherland Miller, remembers hearing the adults around her, particularly Jessie's siblings, speaking of the hardship that Kitchener's parents were having, and donating food, clothing and even a sewing machine to the MacDonald family.

Willard Kitchener MacDonald and his sister Kathleen, circa 1920.
(Photo courtesy of Shirley Sutherland Miller)

The family never seemed to hold onto the charitable donations. There was growing suspicion in those years that much of what Jessie and Howard were receiving was being sold off, possibly to generate money that was being sent away to Unity in the United States, perhaps as donations or simply to pay for all those religious magazines to which Jessie was subscribing on behalf of her family and friends.

Shirley recalls visiting the MacDonald family in the 1940s when she was very young, probably not more than seven or eight, at a small one-and-a-half storey house on Haliburton Road on the outskirts of Pictou. She remembers her Aunt Jessie, sister to Shirley's father Clarence Sutherland, as a very warm and good woman, while Howard was a rather distant man of few words. The house was always full of music.

She says that Kitchener, then a young man, would not show his face until summoned from his attic room down to the kitchen by his father. "I can still see Kitchener's legs coming down through that hole in the ceiling," she says. "Then he would play a piece on his fiddle, and climb right back up to the attic."

Shirley managed to collect a few family photos from this period and put them together in a special album dedicated to her cousin Kitchener. They show Howard, Jessie and their daughter Kathleen as proud and striking people, musical instruments always in hand. While Kitchener played violin and guitar, Kathleen played the piano and organ, pushed to become an accomplished musician by her paternal aunt, Etta Silver.

People who knew the family when they lived in Pictou say Howard played widely throughout the County and also made and sold violins to earn a little money. For years, near the turnoff from the old highway at the entrance to Pictou, a small sign stood that said, "Fiddle Maker."

As for Kitchener's formal education, that remains as mysterious as the family's movements between their return from the United States and the early 1930s, when they showed up to stay for some years near Loganville in Pictou County and then Earltown in Colchester County.

Melvin MacKay knew Kitchener as a young man, when he was working and living in Earltown. Melvin says he always seemed like a "smart and well-educated fellow" who had completed grade eleven, which back in the Depression years was more exceptional than it was the rule in many rural areas of Nova Scotia.

It does seem that at some time in the mid-1930s, the family spent time in Truro before moving into the Gunn House near Loganville in Pictou County.

Coincidentally – or not – this move occurred around the time a third baby appeared in the family. Ronald Howard MacDonald was born in 1935, reportedly in a maternity home in Truro. When he was

Howard MacDonald with Jessie MacDonald (*née* Sutherland) and her mother Hannah Sutherland (seated) holding Ronald MacDonald, circa 1940. (Photo courtesy of Shirley Sutherland Miller.)

Kathleen MacDonald (left), Etta Silver, Howard MacDonald's sister, (back right), Ronald MacDonald, and Jessie MacDonald (seated), circa 1939.
(Photo courtesy of Shirley Sutherland Miller)

brought home to Loganville, he was presented and raised as Howard's and Jessie's third child, younger brother to Kathleen and Kitchener.

Anyone who dared to whisper anything to the contrary or to speculate on the likelihood of Jessie getting pregnant at the age of forty-two, nineteen years after her first son was born – or to make the mistake of saying out loud that they had not seen Jessie pregnant with the third child – was likely to invoke the wrath of MacDonald family friends, who would tolerate no such gossip. Today, however, some who knew the family at the time will say out loud that the new baby was actually Kathleen's son, and grandson to Howard and Jessie.

Jessie's sister, Kitchener's aunt, has memories of Ronnie as a very small boy, which he would have been in the late 1930s, with beautiful curly dark hair, which was unwashed, as was he. He was very poorly dressed, as if his parents were just not able to care for him the way Jessie's siblings felt they should. Or perhaps, as one elderly resident of Pictou says, the neglect may have reflected the fact that he was a child that had initially brought "shame" to the family. Kitchener himself sometimes referred to Ronald as "the one who is supposed to be my brother" and one friend says he used the word "impostor" to refer to his "younger brother."

After the baby was born, Ruth Smith recalls that Howard and Jessie would come down to her parents' farmhouse every day for milk for "baby Ronnie," about the same time that Kitchener started to show up regularly in the kitchen of the Smith family home to play his violin. Ruth's first and very fond memories of Kitchener, when he was eighteen or nineteen just before Ronald was born, were of him sitting in a corner of that comfortable and spacious country kitchen in her parents' farmhouse, playing music – a passion that would last him his entire life.

This was about the same time that Hector MacKenzie recalls getting to know Kitchener a little, although he had seen him at musical evenings all over Pictou County throughout his earlier years.

"In 1936, I was working on a farm in Salt Springs," Hector says. "And I knew Kitchener because he was also working on a farm at

Mount Thom, with the Maxwell family who were friends of his aunt, Mrs. Etta Silver. Well, we were both working on farms, but even then, Kitchener was kind of different. He had a big hound dog, and he would just go off walking in the woods with his dog, disappear from the farm where he was supposed to be working, and he'd forget to come back for a couple of days."

Hector says it's not just hindsight that makes him think Kitchener always had a strong loner streak in him, something that set him apart from the mainstream. He was, even then, something of an enigma. He was someone few people really knew very well, someone who didn't pay much attention to what people thought of him. "He was a wiry guy, just the kind of guy you wouldn't want to wrestle with," says Hector. "He didn't shave every day, or worry about having his hair cut very often, but he wasn't a bad-looking young man."

"He liked the woods, he liked nature. And that was his nature," says Hector. "Even if he hadn't jumped that train, I think he would have ended up in the woods anyway, because he was always a loner."

A loner, but not an antisocial loner, according to those who played music with him and saw him regularly at dances. He attended many of those in West Branch and Earltown, playing the guitar or fiddle, and he worked on and off in various sawmills in the area.

Melvin MacKay can still pull up some colourful and slightly ribald memories of the years they worked and played together near East Earltown. Melvin says that Kitchener, like his father Howard, wasn't cut out for the daily grind, not one to stick to hard or dull work for very long. He recalls setting off to work with Kitchener in the Sutherland mill, near the community of Nuttby, to spend the day doing the backbreaking job of carrying sawed fir boards, or deal. After a couple of hours Melvin says he looked around and noticed Kitchener was nowhere to be seen; he had already abandoned the work, headed down to the office for his pay and gone off into the woods on his own.

Melvin and Kitchener didn't just work together in the mills, though. For a while they also lived together in a camp in East Earltown. They earned a little money bootlegging, making home brew out of brown sugar and molasses, "pretty strong stuff," says MacKay, not like today's watery beer with a paltry five percent alcohol.

"He had a good sense of humour," says Melvin, "as long as the joke was on someone else, and not on him. He couldn't stand that. He was a quiet man, but if anybody picked on him, he could get pretty wild."

He says at one time, Kitchener was considered to be the strongest man in the area, and although he wasn't a violent man, he did get into the occasional scrap, not uncommon at dances when the moonshine was flowing.

Melvin, like another of Kitchener's contemporaries in Earltown, Viola Wall (*née* Murphy), says Kitchener didn't give the impression of being a ladies' man and neither can recall him ever even dancing with a girl at any of the dances where he played guitar and fiddle. He may have had his secret rendezvous with girls, but Melvin figures Kitchener could never have stayed with a woman, any more than he himself could. Asked if he ever married, Melvin MacKay, at age eighty-nine, replies, "Not yet."

Hector MacKenzie figures that just because Kitchener lived alone in the woods without women for decades there was no reason to believe he didn't like them. "He liked women, sure he did, and he did without them most of this life," he says. "But he knew what they were there for." His laughter, as he says this, nearly rocks him right off the kitchen chair.

Chapter 3
A man with no ties

We come now to the very complex and mysterious subject of Kitchener's love life, at least back when he seems to have had one before he took to the hills and abandoned all social niceties – hygiene and grooming, for example – altogether. This is a subject, one of many personal ones, that Kitchener just would not discuss, and if he did, it was in confidence with friends who intend to keep it that way or with people who have long since passed away.

During one visit with him on a frosty autumn day in October, 1982, Lloyd Bogle and the friends he had taken with him to Gully Lake for an afternoon jamboree were discussing among themselves what time their respective wives expected them back. It was one of several jam sessions that Lloyd recorded on a small cassette machine with a built-in microphone that caught only some of what was played, said and done that day.

But for some reason, that off-the-cuff exchange about the merits of having a wife at home waiting patiently – or impatiently – for a husband was caught clear as a bell on the cassette tape.

"Well, that's one thing you don't have to worry about, Kitchener," said Lloyd. "You got no wife up here bothering you, getting in your way."

Kitchener's response was almost instant, which was rare, given that he usually took his time responding to an on-going conversation, mulling over his thoughts before airing them, and as often as not changing the subject altogether to show that he had no interest in pursuing a particular subject or replying to a particular question. Not this time. "That's something I never regretted and I never will," Kitchener said emphatically.

His private life and his emotions were not subjects that Kitchener spoke about willingly, if at all. He was like many of his generation, for whom personal lives and inner lives were believed to be just that – *personal* and *inner*, not for public consumption or display. This was a period when public shows of affection between lovers were still very much taboo in rural communities. The legacy of Queen Victoria and the aversion she developed in her later life to all matters sexual, sensual or even emotional, were still very potent forces suppressing talk about these things, even if the Victorian mentality was still no match when it came to controlling all the actual urges. Most churches and the communities that filled the pews each Sunday were still very strict on all matters concerning procreation and marriage. Even if it happened all the time, pregnancy in unmarried young women or teenagers was severely frowned on. With the birth control pill still many years off, every sexual encounter out of wedlock was a kind of Russian roulette. The difference was that it might result not in death but a new life unsanctioned by marriage, which could be awkward in a small and very correct, upstanding and church-going rural community.

As a result, everything personal was shrouded in secrecy, covered up like the proverbial piano legs – with unplanned pregnancies in unmarried girls and romantic liaisons topping the list, especially if the parents on both sides did not approve of a match. Such social ills that today spawn headlines, such as incest or sexual assault, simply *did not exist* – officially, that is, no matter how many people knew and whispered about them. The need for public propriety led to all sorts of private agonies and genealogical gymnastics: grandparents pretending to be a child's parents, for example. Parents who felt shamed by their own daughters (who always seemed to take the blame, as if they had got pregnant on their own) could mete out some unpleasant punishments and ostracism. These were different times, especially in rural areas where there was much propriety and so little privacy.

Even today, half a century later, it is still very difficult to unravel the truth of who was who, who begot whom, and who went with whom back in those years when Kitchener was a young and eligible bachelor. Many memories have faded, many of those involved have long since passed away, and many of those still living are just not keen to talk about what was going on in the woods or out behind the sawmill or barn in those days.

So the facts about Kitchener's love life remain sketchy, to say the very least.

However, it is possible to piece together a few glimpses of the man as he was in the late 1930s. Viola Wall was about to be married herself in those days, and living with her parents in Berichan, between Loganville and Earltown. She remembers Kitchener as a "very nice young man" who played a fine fiddle and guitar in homes and dances in the area around Earltown. He was a close friend to her brothers and a frequent visitor to her family home. She recalls that she often went off with her brothers and Kitchener into the hills to coast on sleighs or to hunt rabbits in the woods, which they cooked up themselves to eat and to feed to the foxes that her father raised.

Viola was also a friend to Edna Marshall, a young woman who lived in the area with her parents, Daniel and Margaret Marshall, in a "camp" – the term used for the draughty tarpaper shacks of ill-fitting boards that served as homes to many people in the area during the Depression, right through World War II and into the 1950s. The Marshall camp was close to the Sutherland sawmill that stood near the remarkable and much-photographed Nuttby farmhouse on what is now the 311 Highway. Unlike the long-gone sawmill, the "Nuttby house" has lived on to become a local landmark, refusing to fall down, built as it was in 1892 by George Lynch to withstand more than a century of howling winds and blizzards on that exposed ridge south of Earltown.

In the late 1930s, Edna was working for her uncle, Henry Marshall, at a sawmill he owned near MacIntosh Lake, not far from Gully Lake in the hills east of Earltown. As fate would have it, the strapping, and according to some, goodlooking young man of music, Willard Kitchener MacDonald, was also working in the MacIntosh Lake sawmill. And it was here, according to Viola, that Kitchener met Edna Marshall. In the way of small rural communities, everyone seemed to know when Edna became pregnant that Kitchener was involved, even if no one ever stated the obvious out loud – certainly not Edna or Kitchener.

"Edna worked all the way through her pregnancy," says Viola Wall. "But she never talked about it. Never let on who was the father."

On September 22, 1939, Edna Marshall gave birth to a baby boy, whom she named Leroy Marshall. She promptly handed her son over to her mother, Margaret Marshall, to raise. Edna was not, as Leroy puts it, a "good mother" to him in those days and indeed she didn't seem to want to have anything to do with her son; she didn't even get around to registering his birth until March, 1947.

"My grandmother looked after me and my uncles," says Leroy, who speaks very fondly of his maternal grandmother as a "very good woman." But he says life was very difficult for her. She had seventeen children to feed in that rustic camp near Nuttby.

Later, in 1950, Margaret and Daniel Marshall would move to East Mountain, closer to Truro, where Leroy's mother Edna had started to work at the Stanfield's clothing factory. Leroy went with them, but three years later he would leave school and head off into the woods to work, which is what he is still doing almost half a century later.

But in his early years, he lived with his grandmother, attended the United Church with her, and tried to steer clear of his mother's temper, which he said could be "wicked."

"My mother was kind of hard to talk to," he says. "She was something similar to Willard and never would talk much, or tell you much of anything personal. And she never looked after me. My grandmother took care of me. In later years she [my mother] started to get more mother-like, but in younger years she never took care of me or looked after me."

Leroy, master of the understatement, continues, "It was quite hard, you know, to get by. But I managed it."

He saw Kitchener frequently when he was a child, without knowing for years that this was his father. His grandparents' camp, where he spent the first eleven years of his life, was just two kilometres up the road from the camp that Kitchener's family called home after they moved there from Loganville in the late 1930s or early 1940s. The MacDonald camp was on the long hill leading from Earltown up to Nuttby Mountain, a stretch of road known as Jack Gunn's Hill, after one of Howard's maternal uncles.

But when he was a small child living with his grandparents and a mother who didn't seem very keen on that role, Leroy says he never saw any evidence that Edna Marshall and Willard Kitchener MacDonald had anything more to do with each other. "They didn't associate in any way, that I know anyway," he says. "My grandmother didn't get along so well with Willard. The rest, well, I wouldn't want to tell you like."

Chapter 4
Troop train jumper

Meanwhile, far from Earltown, World War II was raging on the fighting fields in Europe. Despite early promises by Canada's Prime Minister, William Lyon MacKenzie King, that there would be no conscription, in 1940 the *National Resources Mobilization Act* was passed, allowing the government to call up men for service – but for service only within Canada.

Heavy casualties in Europe and falling numbers of voluntary recruits led to pressure on the government to step up the war effort and MacKenzie King called a plebiscite in 1942, seeking a release from any restrictions on how men were recruited for military service. Quebec voted massively against conscription but the eight provinces with anglophone majorities voted in favour of the release, and MacKenzie King then amended the *National Resources Mobilization Act* to allow the government to send conscripts anywhere it wished.

However, it wasn't until late 1944, when the stream of voluntary enlistments was drying up, that the Canadian government decided to use those controversial powers and send the first conscripts overseas. These men were known disparagingly as "zombies" by their colleagues who had signed up voluntarily for military service. On

November 23, 1944, the House of Commons authorized the dispatch of sixteen thousand of the conscripted men for active duty in Europe, and the first of these soldiers sailed from Halifax on January 3, 1945.

Although little is said about this in most historical accounts of Canada's involvement in the war, with their focus instead on the enormous courage and heroic efforts of Canadian soldiers in liberating Europe from Nazi occupation, the truth is that Kitchener's decision to desert was not all that unusual.

The decision to send conscripted men overseas caused a huge wave of similar desertions. On January 20, 1945, the Government of Canada admitted that 7,800 conscripts had at one time been overdue or absent without leave and that up to that day, 6,300 – more than a third of all those to be sent overseas – were still absent from the training camps to which they had been called.

There is a delay of twenty years after the death of an ex-serviceman before his military records can be made public, so it will not be until 2023 that details about how Kitchener came to be in the army, whether he enlisted or was conscripted under the *National Resources Mobilization Act*, can be accessed by non-relatives. Nevertheless, given that he did leap from a troop train to avoid going to war, it does seem likely that he was a conscript, and unless he was on a train being sent for training somewhere, that his desertion occurred after the government decision of November 1944 to round up sixteen thousand conscripts and send them into action.

Some of his old friends, such as Ruth Smith, think it was earlier than this, probably in 1941 or '42, which it well may have been if he had been conscripted when the *National Resources Mobilization Act* was passed in 1940. But if that is the case, it is unlikely he would have been on a troop train heading off to war. Rather, he would have been headed to a training camp or to a military position within Canada, and not to Halifax for a ship taking him overseas for duty.

The actual details of how he came to be conscripted – if he was – or even on that troop train, let alone how and why he got off it, are elusive at best, downright confusing and contradictory at worst. First, it was a subject he refused point-blank to talk about, not even to his closest lifelong friends. Then there is the bothersome question of his nationality. The Smith family in Loganville maintain that the Canadian government had no business even calling Willard up for service, given that he was born in the United States and, to the best of their knowledge, he was never naturalized as a Canadian citizen.

There are many conflicting versions of when, where and how Willard jumped the train then managed to evade capture in the weeks and months afterwards. David Smith and his mother, Ruth, say the story they heard was that he had jumped off on the old rail line near Riversdale in Colchester County.

Lloyd Bogle, who befriended Kitchener in 1971, thinks it happened at the end of the North River Road, not far from Truro. And Ed Lorraine, former Warden of Colchester County and later the MLA for the constituency, says that around his farm in Onslow, people believe Kitchener jumped where the train slows to cross the North River on its way into Truro from Amherst.

Hector MacKenzie, who had been working with Kitchener on farms around Mount Thom before the war, had already signed up and gone off for training when Kitchener deserted. But he is fairly sure that he got off the train at Campbell's Siding, not far from Central West River. Hector also figures that Kitchener's mother Jessie was well aware that her son was going to hop off the train taking him to war, and may even have been part of the plan before it happened.

Lloyd MacIntosh believes Kitchener was conscripted and says the story he always heard was that he was coming back from his last leave, and about to be sent overseas, when he disembarked at West River Station, very close to Campbell's Siding and Mount Thom, an area Kitchener knew very well indeed.

Viola Wall's brother Arthur Murphy accompanied Kitchener to the station to see him off, but she can't recall what year that was or where it was he boarded. Arthur Murphy would eventually go overseas and come home scarred by the horrors he witnessed in Europe.

"Arthur never talked about the war," says Viola. "I know he said he was very hurt by the suffering of the children he saw in the war, and it was too much for him. He died when he was only forty-five. It was too much, too much."

But she says there were no hard feelings between her brother, who went to the war, and Kitchener, who didn't. She says that even if Willard Kitchener MacDonald was hiding away for fear of capture, he still made his way down from his hideout in the woods to her family home near West Branch to play music in the years after the war.

And Viola, like Melvin MacKay, thinks that the jump occurred in Wentworth Valley, perhaps near Folly Lake. Melvin recalls that Kitchener had been called up and that he was sent for training in Aldershot, near Kentville in the Annapolis Valley.

Melvin MacKay was sent overseas to war in 1944 and didn't return to Canada until 1946. He says he wasn't on the train with Willard, but he does remember that another man from Earltown who jumped off the same train, Johnny MacKay, was apprehended by the authorities about a week after he deserted and sent down to McNab's Island in Halifax Harbour, where "they darn near killed him."

Lloyd MacIntosh says a third man, Johnny MacKay's brother Hector, also leapt from the same train, but doesn't recall what happened to him.

On his return from the war in 1946, Melvin went straight back to work in the woods and says he saw a lot of Kitchener in the late 1940s and early 1950s. Although Kitchener may well have been in hiding from the authorities and fearing capture for having deserted, he remained in the camp on Jack Gunn's Hill, elusive perhaps but clearly not in hiding from many people in the community. One elderly farmer in the area recalls working with him briefly at the Sutherland mill in the late 1940s – briefly because one day a military jeep pulled up in front of the mill and Kitchener bolted.

Still, Lloyd MacIntosh, who figures he knew Kitchener as well as anyone, says, "I'm not sure they ever really wanted to catch Willard. But he might have thought they did."

Although the death penalty for desertion was still on the books during World War II, it was never carried out, with the only exception being the very controversial execution in Italy on July 5, 1945, of

Private Harold Joseph Pringle, an absentee soldier who was convicted by a general court martial after being charged with the murder of a fellow soldier. Several recent books have offered compelling evidence that Pringle was innocent of that murder and that this execution – the last one of any Canadian soldier – was a miscarriage of military justice.

However, that did not mean that deserters were let off easily if caught, even if they deserted before leaving Canada. Most were forced to do heavy labour, and were treated poorly given the prevailing views at the time on their lack of patriotism – or their "cowardice." Nor was conscientious objection much of an option during World War II, as so many pacifist groups – Quakers, Doukabors and Mennonites – found out when they refused to show up for duty and were imprisoned. In western Canada, many of these groups were eventually enlisted into "alternative" service that included farm work, when the federal government passed an Order-in-Council in 1943, to help compensate for the loss of farm labour during the war. But there is no sign that Kitchener ever sought to be labelled a conscientious objector, or that he participated in the Farm Duty Plan that permitted military trainees and servicemen to work as agricultural labourers for relatively elevated daily rates.

Even if he did manage to avoid court martial and the heavy labour he would have undergone had he been apprehended in the years immediately after the war, that didn't mean he didn't pay for his desertion. Life was not at all easy in rural Canada in those postwar years, especially in chronically impoverished areas such as northern Nova Scotia. There, most people still eked their living out of the land, performing the backbreaking work of the family farmer, or in the woods wielding an axe and heaving logs, or at sawmills, carrying heavy planks, which was poorly paid and very hard work – akin to "slavery" according to Lloyd Bogle. But in choosing the "freedom" of self-imposed exile from the mainstream, Kitchener also chose a very hard life of isolation in extremely difficult living conditions.

Ruth Smith's interpretation of his decision to desert was simply that "he was too peaceful to bother going to war."

Melvin MacKay's take on it differs a little. "He told me he hated killing," Melvin says with his characteristic laugh. "I think he was afraid; I don't think he hated killing people. He was scared."

Some in the Earltown area who recall friends and family members who did go to war and never returned say that there was some resentment in the community about Kitchener's "shirking" of his military duty, especially in later years when his fame grew and the media began to treat him as a kind of folk hero. "He was no hero," says one elderly man. "Others went to war and died, and others worked hard their whole lives to make a living and suffered much of the same hardship that Willard did despite their hard work. What he did by moving into the woods was not easy but it wasn't heroic either."

All Kitchener would say about his desertion is that it says in the Bible "Thou shalt not kill" and that he "didn't like to kill anyone." And no matter how many times people informed him that the government had declared an amnesty on deserters in 1950, he either refused to believe it, or by the time he learned of it, had become so used to the solitude of his life in the woods that he had no interest in trying to re-insert himself into a rapidly changing world.

Ed Lorraine says he had the impression when he went to visit with Kitchener in the 1970s and '80s that he still didn't realize the war was over, certainly didn't believe there was an amnesty and lived in fear that "they'd come and get him." Those who considered Kitchener a friend in later life and even those who had known him most of his life rarely asked him for details of this period, respecting his privacy. And those who did were gently reprimanded with silence or a quiet changing of the subject.

So when, exactly, he moved into the woods to stay – whether it was immediately after he leapt from the train or a gradual process after that and into the 1950s – remains very much open to discussion and part of his mystery.

Chapter 5
A troubled family

Leroy Marshall says that during most of the war, Kitchener's family was living in the camp on Jack Gunn's Hill near Earltown. During that time, the family of Vonetta Mae Chouinard (*née* Stevens) was living in the small, one-and-a-half storey house off Haliburton Road in Pictou, which they were renting from Kitchener's father, Howard MacDonald.

In her self-published book, *Vonetta's Memoirs of Beautiful Nova Scotia*, Vonetta paints poignant pictures of how difficult life was during the Dirty Thirties, and how it drove many families to move about seeking employment in the woods to avoid starvation. In 1938, at the age of three, she moved with her grandparents to camps in Earltown. When the war broke out and her grandfather went to work at the military base in Debert, the family moved to Masstown. In 1942 they relocated again, this time to Pictou, where her grandfather had work in the shipyards thriving with wartime business. There, they moved into the house on Haliburton Road.

Howard had bought this house in the late 1930s from the late Lester Clarke. Lester's wife Lillian says her husband had built the house in 1934 or 1935 on two acres of land that had been carved off the larger Glenalmond Estate, which had been shared between

Lester and his brother Byron. But Lillian Clarke says the house rapidly became too small for herself and her husband by the time they had three small sons; it had only one true bedroom and a "so-called pantry" that they had turned into a second bedroom for the children.

Lester Clarke then sold the house and the two-acre lot to Howard for four hundred dollars, and the MacDonald family moved in, probably in the very late 1930s after they left Loganville, when Ronald was still a toddler. Before buying Lester's house, Lillian says the MacDonalds had been living in a large rented house up the road a few kilometres, in Lyons Brook, between Pictou and Scotsburn. Lillian doesn't know how the MacDonald family came up with the money to buy the house, given how much they seem to have struggled financially over the years, moving about gypsy-style, staying in houses belonging to Howard's uncles in Loganville and Earltown on and off during the 1930s and 1940s.

Lillian recalls that the MacDonalds used old newspapers as wallpaper to insulate the inside walls of the small house. She doesn't recall Howard ever working at a regular job, or Kitchener either. Her memories of Kitchener, who would have been in his early twenties at the end of the 1930s, are vague: an elusive man who traipsed about in a big, heavy coat that reached his ankles. She recalls Jessie as trim and petite, very well turned out, despite the family's apparent poverty. There was always some talk about wealthy relatives in the United States. Lillian says Kathleen was a very pretty young woman with lovely auburn hair, but adds that the family kept to themselves and no one really seemed to know them well.

Vonetta lived in the MacDonalds' house from 1942 until 1948. During those years Howard and Jessie would come by once a month, often with Kitchener, Kathleen and Ronald in tow, to collect the rent money.

The house had one big bedroom off the kitchen, a small living room, an open front sunporch, electricity and an attic that could also serve as a bedroom and apparently did when Kitchener was staying there. Vonetta says her family fetched water from a spring, and recalls that the yard was full of magnificent cherry trees that filled with blossoms each spring.

She recalls Kitchener's father, whom she knew only as Fiddle Foot, as a magnificent violin player. She says he owned a Stradivarius and was a "quiet" and "very nice" man. She doesn't remember Kitchener as particularly goodlooking, perhaps because he was, as Hector McKenzie says, even then somewhat unkempt.

Vonetta has clear memories of going through the rubbish pile the MacDonald family had left behind when they vacated the house in 1942. She was greatly impressed by the numbers of pairs of shoes, and especially the huge size of Fiddle Foot's shoes — which she guesses must have been fourteen or even eighteen.

Vonetta's family left the house in 1948, the year the MacDonald family — minus Kitchener — moved back to Pictou to settle in their own house, where they would stay till the 1960s. The property was flanked on one side by the large Glenalmond Farm belonging to Byron Clarke and on the other by the farm belonging to the Humphreys family.

Bud Humphreys was in his late teens when the MacDonalds moved back to Pictou, and he remembers them as "excellent neighbours" in the sense that they "never did anybody any harm." But he also says they were "distant." When the wind knocked down a signboard in front of their house Howard MacDonald unfairly blamed the local boys for it. He says the family never had any money, and Howard drove almost every day to town on his bicycle. Bud's clearest and best memories are of Ronald MacDonald, same age as he was, who often came across the fields to the Humphreys' farm to play music with him. Ronald seemed proud of Kitchener and often made a point of saying that he had learned a particular violin piece from his older brother. Ronald was already an excellent fiddler.

Bud vividly remembers a fire in the house in the early 1960s, when he went over to help out while the fire department muddled rather ineffectually with the hose and water, unable to control the blaze until it had badly gutted the house. He says Howard moved all the family's belongings out of the house and then sat out front on a chair while the firemen slowly brought the flames under control. Although neighbours offered the MacDonalds an alternate residence, they preferred to move back into their house after the fire. There they stayed until the property was expropriated in the mid-1960s to make way for the new causeway that was opened in 1968, linking Brown's Point and Abercrombie, where the pulp mill had begun operation the previous year. Howard sold the actual house, which was moved to Scotch Hill near Pictou. It is still standing and inhabited today, looking shipshape with new vinyl siding but without the small front porch of yesteryear.

Anyone coming around the Pictou rotary and heading towards New Glasgow on the Trans-Canada Highway today is actually driving over what was once the land that belonged to Kitchener's father. The Glenalmond farm has been swallowed up by an enormous, impressive private estate of sumptuous groomed lawns, overlooking West River and across to that monstrous fume-belching pulp mill on Abercrombie Point on the far side of that otherwise lovely body of water and its environs.

People in Pictou who remember the family all agree that the MacDonalds kept very much to themselves, perhaps because of their religion. Their faith probably isolated them socially; Unity had no church in Pictou or even in eastern Canada, and no one is able to recall ever seeing them in any other church that might have drawn them into the community.

"They liked to give the impression they weren't very smart people," says one elderly woman who knew them in Pictou. "But they were; they were smart."

Beth Henderson (*née* Clarke and niece to Lillian Clarke) grew up on the Glenalmond farm right next door to the MacDonald family home. She would have been just five years old in 1948, the year that Howard, Jessie, Kathleen and Ronald moved back into their house to stay. Beth has very clear recollections of Howard, whom she describes as a "gracious man, a gentleman, who spoke only when he had to," a physically imposing man despite his posture, always a little "bent over," with a large nose and chin, a thin mouth and very large feet.

"I remember the sounds of the violin wafting down over that hill on summer nights," says Beth. "I believe he studied at the Boston Conservatory."

As a teenager, Beth worked at Johnny's Canteen in Pictou, which today has become a convenience store at the entrance to the town, not far from the Sobeys shopping complex situated just off the rotary. "Howard seemed quite elderly then, but he would come by the canteen on his bicycle. He was very fussy about what he ate. He always took the same things. He would only eat Husky brown bread and brown eggs and [drink only] Pepsi. He was very health conscious."

It seems to have been in the late 1940s that Kitchener's sister Kathleen fell ill, and the family went through a very difficult time. Mildred Adamson is a former teacher in Pictou, born in 1913, who has clear memories of the Great Depression, the war years and the never-ending hardship of life in northern Nova Scotia even after the Second World War. She grew up on a farm in the area, and in the 1930s her family staved off hunger by raising cows, pigs and chickens, and producing their own vegetables. There was no money at all, she remembers, and people lived very simply, "not all that different from the way that Willard lived his entire life." Her own husband had signed up for duty and gone overseas in 1940, and been taken prisoner of war in 1945. "They nearly starved them to death," she says. "My husband learned never to be fussy about food again."

By contrast, she remembers hearing about the distinctive dietary habits in the MacDonald household in the years following the war, which may have been related to their Unity faith, a very powerful influence on their lives.

"Howard was a very religious man," says Mildred. "My son-in-law took his violin to him to have it fixed," she says. "And on the inside he wrote something about music and God."

"Kathleen, the daughter, had mental health problems," Mildred continues. And the nurses who looked after Kitchener's sister in Pictou attributed her mental illness in part to the diet she had been prescribed at home, which involved a lot of turnip juice. Some say she was also locked up in her room.

Leroy Marshall says his grandmother Jessie was not a believer in pills, and that she had her own idea of what constituted healthy food and medicine, which did nothing to cure Kathleen. There are conflicting views on what illness she might have had that rendered her bedridden in the first place. Some say tuberculosis. Others think diabetes or cancer. Another factor may have been the tension that marred relations between Jessie and her sister-in-law, Etta, who reportedly wished to push Kathleen into a serious musical career. Some suspect Kathleen may have been profoundly troubled by the family arrangement and the public pretence of having everyone believe the child in the family was her younger brother rather than her son. There are also some deeply unsettling allegations about who may have fathered the child, none of which can be substantiated now. If true, however, they could certainly have contributed to Kathleen's mental breakdown, especially in a family with strict religious principles and at a time when public pride and the fear of public shame could drive people to extreme and extraordinary behaviours.

Whatever it was that ailed Kathleen took its toll on her mother's health as well. Beth Henderson's memories of Jessie in those post-war years were of someone quite ill. "I would say Mrs. MacDonald had a nervous breakdown," she says. "She would come over to our house and slip notes under our door. I remember one said, 'The brass buttons are watching you.'" Jessie would also come over regularly to get turnips from Beth's father, which she then squeezed to get the juice she had prescribed for her daughter.

Like Mildred Adamson, Beth recalls Jessie and her daughter going off to the Nova Scotia Hospital in Dartmouth, while others say they went to the Riverton Home near Stellarton. Wherever it was they went for care, only Jessie came home. Some think Kathleen was buried in the family plot in the Durham Cemetery. But there is no record of her on the headstone on the MacDonald plot, where Kitchener's parents are now buried. Lillian Clarke believes Kathleen was buried "out in the country."

One of the pallbearers at Kathleen's funeral in Pictou, Bobby Watt, cannot recall the exact year of her death but guesses it would have been in the late 1940s when he was in his late teens. He thinks

Kathleen would have been in her late twenties when she passed away. But where she is buried remains a mystery, and the funeral home in Pictou that Bobby Watt believes held the service has no record of one for Kathleen MacDonald in the 1940s or 1950s.

After Kathleen's death, her mother appears to have recovered. Beth Henderson recalls Jessie coming into the bank in Pictou where she worked, "dressed like a real lady, to the nines. And when I told her how good she looked, she would tell me that her clothes were sent to her from the United States."

How much of this family trauma – the illness and death of his sister Kathleen and the nervous problems and recovery of his mother Jessie – Kitchener was there to share and how much it would have implicated or affected him remain very big and unanswerable questions.

Some who befriended him in later years would ask him about his family and be told, "They're all gone," even though this was in the 1970s when his mother was still alive. After their land on Haliburton Road was expropriated in the 1960s, Jessie and Howard lived with Ronald MacDonald and his wife in a house they had built at Loch Broom, just across West River from their former home – Howard until he died in 1971 and Jessie till 1980, when she spent a few months in a seniors' home before her death.

Robert Clark became acquainted with the MacDonald family in the early 1950s, when he worked with Ronald MacDonald, eight years his senior, haying on farms around Pictou. He says in these years Kitchener would still come over from the Earltown area on his bicycle to visit the family. Then, from the late 1950s until 1979, Jessie would hire Robert to drive her into the woods to see her son.

He says that up to the late 1960s, Kitchener was living in that same old camp on Jack Gunn's Hill that had been his base for years. It was not until the end of that decade that he moved to the hut at Gully Lake, saying he wanted to get further away from the 311 highway and the noise of passing cars.

Robert Clark says Jessie usually took bags and envelopes to her son, and guesses she sometimes gave him a little money. On other occasions Robert would drive Jessie and Kitchener down to the general stores in Earltown to do some shopping for heavy items such as potatoes. He also took Jessie to Moncton a few times to visit with her sister.

Until she grew frail in the 1970s, Robert took Jessie out to see Kitchener about once a month. And on each occasion, she asked her son to come out to live with the family – which in the 1950s and early 1960s would have been in Pictou and in the late 1960s and 1970s would have been in the house Jessie and Howard shared with Ronald and his wife in Loch Broom. Kitchener's unchanging response to his mother's pleas to move out of the woods would be a polite and non-committal, "I'd have to think about it."

Robert says Jessie was terrified of bears and never liked to make her way alone over the rough territory to the camp on Jack Gunn's Hill and later at Gully Lake. She would often wait in the vehicle while either he or someone else went in to fetch Kitchener, who would escort her in to his camp. She was a petite woman, not much taller than five feet tall according to Robert, but with her son escorting her, she would still insist on crossing the brooks and clambering over boulders to get to her son's woodland homes. Even when she was in her eighties, he says she would climb in through the tiny window of the Gully Lake shack – just as Kitchener himself would be doing as an octogenarian.

Lloyd Bogle had the impression that Kitchener was very fond of his mother and often said if he had money he would do something special for her, but didn't specify what that would be.

So it does seem strange to many, especially those who knew Kitchener to be very close to his mother, that he would suggest to visitors that he had no living family or relatives – unless this was just a polite way to keep his private affairs private. The headstone in Durham Cemetery shows three people are buried there – Kitchener's father Howard (1885–1971), his mother Jessie (1893–1980) and Annie Laura MacDonald (1878–1957), sister to Howard.

It also confounds those close to the family that in 1980 when his mother died and a friend of the family offered to take Kitchener out to the funeral, he refused to go. One of his oldest friends suggests that Kitchener was "cross" with his family for some reason that will never be known. And yet, both his mother and later Ronald went out to visit him regularly.

Friends say Ronald MacDonald was a master fiddler who played at dances all over the province with his wife, also an accomplished musician and on whom "Ronnie doted." He died in 2001 at the age of sixty-six, and is buried not far from Durham in the Gladstone Cemetery at Four Mile Brook, along with his wife, who died in 1997. Robert Clark says Kitchener refused to believe that Ronald had died, and refused to come out for the funeral, just as he had for his mother's in 1980.

As a neighbour to the MacDonalds when she was growing up on Glenalmond Farm on the outskirts of Pictou, Beth Henderson has clear and fond memories of Ronald, whom everyone called Ronnie. Kitchener was twenty-six years her senior, but she was just eight years younger than Ronnie and he taught her how to tune a guitar and also took her to see Johnny Cash when he performed in New Glasgow.

Kitchener was far more elusive. Beth doesn't remember seeing him when she was a very young girl in the late 1940s but does have memories from her teenage years in the late 1950s when he was still coming out of the woods to visit with his parents in Pictou from time to time.

"He was very musical and he played the guitar," she says. "He had a very long thumb nail that he used as a pick. But no matter how fast the piece was we were playing, he kept the same slow rhythm."

Beth remembers going to beach parties in 1957 and there she also remembers Kitchener. "He used to go to Waterside Beach with us to beach parties," she says. "Where he wanted to go, he went."

"He didn't seem used to mixed company. The boys used to tease him by dragging him out in the water and trying to pull his trunks down because there were girls there. He had borrowed a pair of swimming trunks. He always seemed to lap up the attention."

Beach parties on the Northumberland Strait? Swimming? Music on the beach? None of this seems to reconcile itself with the legend of the man the outside world came to know as "The Hermit" who had gone into hiding supposedly for fear of capture by the military police.

Beth smiles at that legend, at all the articles and documentaries in the media that over the years painted the picture of the inscrutable recluse of Gully Lake, juxtaposed against her memories of the fiddle-playing man she called Willard.

"When I saw all those articles, I thought to myself, 'What's wrong with this picture?'" says Beth, with a laugh. "I think he loved all the attention, even if he didn't go looking for it."

Chapter 6
Speak but little, trust but few

The mythology that developed around Kitchener in recent years presents a true conundrum to the writer trying to sift through it all to sort fact from folklore, to separate the man from the legend. According to that legend, the bare bones of the story as told within the community and later across the country in news reports, he moved back to Gully Lake after jumping that train, and stayed there living as a hermit for sixty years, a complete recluse living in a time warp, never believing the war was over, never believing that "they" were not coming to get him.

There may be nothing wrong with that legend, except that it is at odds with some important facts. For one, Kitchener didn't move to Gully Lake until the late 1960s, and certainly didn't entirely disappear from public view and social events immediately after he deserted, as was often assumed.

In the early years after the war and throughout the 1950s, he lived primarily in his rustic camp on Jack Gunn's Hill, just a few kilometres from Earltown. He moved about a great deal, mostly on a bicycle, probably had other camps in the woods of the area, and was seen frequently in and around Earltown. He played at dances and he visited with friends in the area, and also made his way to Pictou to visit his parents and, as Beth Henderson attests, even went to beach parties.

It was only at the end of the 1950s, or even late in the 1960s after he shifted his permanent home to Gully Lake, that he stopped visiting his family in Pictou.

Ruth Smith has very fond memories of the friendly man who graced the kitchen of her family home right through all those years when he was "in hiding." Although he never stayed overnight, always preferring to go "home" to his camps in the woods, he did come down to visit and she says he wrestled and romped with her children.

"The children never liked to see him leave," says Ruth. "He would tell them all sorts of stories about animals and birds. And when he left, they would all complain and ask him when he was coming back. And he would say to them, 'I'll send you a message on the wing of a bird.' He always said he was going to come back as a bird, a blue jay or a crow. He liked those birds."

Her son David Smith spent a lot of time over the years up in the woods around Gully Lake with his friend. He says Kitchener moved about a lot, just as he had done throughout his early years with his nomadic parents. He stayed in very crude dug-outs and lean-tos, and sometimes even slept in trees for fear of being trampled by moose during the night.

Kitchener would make moonshine out of berries and whatever else he could get his hands on that would ferment. Then he would make his way down the trails on the north side of Gully Lake, riding his bicycle, with the bottles clinking in the front carrier as he came tearing down the hill, making the dust fly on what is known as Gunshot Road.

He also made soap to sell, using hardwood ashes and leaching the lye from them and bringing his concoction down the hill to peddle, but as one friend says with a laugh, "Of course, he never used the soap himself."

"On foot it took him about two and a half hours to get down from Gully Lake," says Ruth Smith. "In the winter he came out on skis and snowshoes, and he was always determined he was going to pay me for the few things I gave him and I said no, 'Willard, you're a neighbour. A neighbour and a friend don't do those kinds of things.'"

"His favourite was my biscuits and jelly," she says. "He liked porridge and he liked stew and a bucket of salt herring every winter. He would take a little sugar but he wasn't a great sugar person."

"One day I was cooking and he had a few drinks and he was sitting beside my husband Frank on the couch and Willard was bugging me. I was baking and when I took the cookies out of the oven I said, 'Willard, if you don't shut your damn mouth I'll throw these cookies at you.' And I went to the pantry with them and Willard said, 'Oh Frankie, there's nothing like the wrath of a red-haired woman.'"

Ruth's infectious laugh fills the kitchen as she tells this story, a country kitchen still smelling of – and full of – fresh-baked biscuits and cookies. She serves these up to visitors, along with genuine rural hospitality and jars of delectable green jelly made from mint plants she collects from the banks of the stream that passes through the farm.

"There was something he always told my children and I think it's something that he followed himself," she says. "He liked to tell them, 'Speak but little, trust but few, but always paddle your own canoe.'"

Leroy Marshall recalls very clearly the day in 1953, when he was fourteen years old and Kitchener would have been thirty-seven, that his father approached him for the very first time, not to acknowledge any blood relationship but just to talk.

"I knew who he was," says Leroy. "I was surprised to see him; I wasn't expecting him or anything. I was working at a sawmill in back of the Archibald Clearing in Kemptown. I was working for Donnie Lynch, and he and Willard was great friends. They lived just a short piece from each other. Donnie told me Willard was my father. I didn't know what he was going to say, though. He talked real good. He was talking to me quite a bit until Joe MacLellan showed up and they didn't get along for some reason, and he left just like that. He could talk good, sensible-like and things. He was quite well educated, or he seemed to be, more so than I am."

Still, Kitchener didn't let on to Leroy that he was his father, and Leroy remained very much on his own throughout his teen years. He says he saw Howard and Jessie MacDonald, his grandparents, a few times but never got to know them.

This meeting of son and father in the sawmill, which occurred eight years after the war had ended and Kitchener had supposedly long since gone into hiding, lends credence to some suggestions that there was more to Leroy's father's decision to move into the woods to live on his own than just fear of capture for desertion.

There are all sorts of possible explanations, none substantiated. There are tales of another child, this time a daughter, who also went unacknowledged and who in fact never wished to be associated with her father. And there are also obscure rumours and allegations about yet another unplanned pregnancy, the result of Kitchener's relationship with one of Leroy's mother's cousins, which is said to have caused a good deal of hard feeling between the two women. Hard feelings that may well have involved Kitchener, and which would not have left him unscathed.

In a CBC television interview, Kitchener quotes someone as once saying to him that he was "a worthless shirt [sic] and no good for nothing." This suggests that somewhere in his past there was some hurt and insult that left its mark on him, enough for him to recall it decades later and repeat it to journalists. It may well be that Kitchener deeply felt the resentment that one elderly resident of the area says existed after the war, when some families in Earltown who were mourning their lost brothers or sons may have let Kitchener know what they thought of his decision to avoid military duty.

There was also a tragic road accident after a dance in West Branch; a girl was struck and killed by a car in which Kitchener was an occupant. This may have caused him much personal agony and perhaps contributed to his increasing need for solitude, spelling the end of his visits to dances to play music in the area.

And in the 1950s or early 1960s, he had at least one very unpleasant brush with the law. At that time there were two general stores in Earltown, one owned by the late Earl MacKay, which Murphy Stonehouse would eventually buy and which would become Kitchener's lifeline for essentials such as flour, potatoes and the special tobacco leaf he wanted ordered in for him. The other one, now closed, belonged to the late Doug MacKay.

David Smith says that when he was very young, the general stores were robbed, although Leroy thinks the robbery was in the store then owned and run by Doug MacKay. The police leapt to the conclusion that there was one obvious culprit – Willard Kitchener MacDonald, and they "marched him off," according to David. One source in the area says that at the time, Kitchener was good friends with a young man being raised as a foster child, who had developed a poor reputation in the community, and this liaison may have led to the incorrect assumption that Kitchener had a hand in the robberies.

Leroy remembers watching the RCMP officer from Tatamagouche leading his father away from Earltown in handcuffs. Kitchener was released almost immediately. This incident must have given him the proof he needed that he was no longer on any wanted list for military deserters. It also suggests that he wasn't really in hiding at that point; otherwise, it seems unlikely the RCMP would have been able to find him.

Nevertheless, such an unpleasant experience with the police probably did little to ease his deep and lifelong mistrust of the authorities. David Smith says that after this incident, Kitchener always referred to Earltown as "Squirreltown."

There is no way of knowing what it was in Willard Kitchener MacDonald that drove him into the woods and then kept him there for decades. And to speculate further on what anguish he may have suffered in his youth in the throes of romantic affairs or troubled by family traumas and secrets, or a fervent desire to avoid the killing fields – and a possible military court martial – would mean moving into the realm of pop psychology and speculation, of which he surely would not approve. What is certain is that he was an intensely private man – "secretive and suspicious," according to Lloyd MacIntosh – who chose a life of solitude for his own private reasons, reasons that he took with him when he departed this world.

In lieu of any explanation that only Kitchener could have offered for his chosen life in the woods, many of his friends and acquaintances have developed their own, based on snippets of his personal life they were able to coax out of him and combined with the impressions – some very contradictory – that he made on them.

Lloyd Bogle sees it as a tragic story of broken love, a romance interrupted by the call to war duty. He abided by the message in the Bible that forbids killing, says Lloyd. "But he paid for it dearly, though, with his lifestyle. Or I think he did."

Melvin MacKay thinks his old friend would have been better off had he not jumped off the troop train. Others say his decision to desert did land him in the woods, on his own, with all the hardship that entailed, but they point out that he might never have returned from the war, perished in battle like so many others.

What is also sure is that Kitchener's early years, like those of most rural Canadians during the Dirty Thirties Depression years, were not filled with any luxuries, or material amenities, so he didn't have to learn to do without these comforts once he did move back into the woods to live. Many older people in the Cobequid Mountains of northern Nova Scotia lived without running water, electricity, modern appliances and indoor plumbing until very recently. In fact, there are some people in the area who still do so to this day.

His early years certainly prepared him for a tougher life than do the childhoods of most Canadians today. He had always loved the woods; he knew how to hunt, fish and trap, had done so his whole life. Indoor plumbing, running water and a soft bed were not things to which he had grown accustomed, or felt he needed. He simply did not require the material comforts most of us in wealthy countries feel we could not live without. Nor did he seek the company of family and friends or crave the social acceptance or professional success that so many of us seem to need to feel contented, fulfilled or even worthwhile. As difficult as it is for many of us to imagine, perhaps he enjoyed the freedom this lifestyle afforded him.

"If he was alone he was happy," says Melvin MacKay. "He didn't want nobody. He didn't seem to want anybody at all."

The Smith family also feels he led the life he wanted. They respected the fact that he alone knew why he was up there and why he stayed there, and that he simply was not interested in the trappings of what we call "the good life."

Lloyd MacIntosh simplifies it still more. "He was different," he says.

Leroy, who like his father has also lived in the woods in hardship over the years, sees it differently. He has never subscribed to the legend that it was the fear of capture for deserting that sent his father into the woods. He says Kitchener didn't really start living like a hermit until much later, at the end of the 1950s, and he sees this as the result of dark personal and family secrets.

"He was his own prisoner," Leroy says of his father. "And he was the only one that had the key."

From left to right: David Smith, Leroy Marshall, Shirley Sutherland Miller, and Ruth Smith, in the Smith kitchen, Loganville, NS. (Photo by Joan Baxter)

Chapter 7
A hermit's home

Some of Kitchener's oldest friends, Ruth Smith, for example, never made their way up to Gully Lake to visit him. Rather, they stayed at home and let Kitchener come down to see them when he wanted their company or was passing through on his bicycle, headed to River John or across to Pictou to sell some pelts from the animals he trapped – muskrat, beaver, mink, otter, fox – or perhaps to distribute a little home brew.

Ruth says that despite what the outside world might think, Kitchener was not the only loner who had taken to a life in the woods around Gully Lake. Another man, Hardy Halbrett, a very skilled mechanic, lived in similar conditions and solitude on Gunshot Road not too far from Gully Lake, coming down to the Smith house to repair the tractor. But unlike Kitchener, Ruth says he would spend the night in their home.

Although David Smith knew Kitchener well from his many visits to their home in Loganville, he was already a teenager before he first saw the hut that had become Kitchener's home at Gully Lake. He and his brother were out hunting when they heard the familiar strains of fiddling, and they followed the melody until they came across their friend and his hut.

Kitchener's hut at Gully Lake, his home for many years until it burned to the ground in May 2003. The window also served as the door.
(Photo by Alan Sullivan)

That was the now-famous little structure, six by eight feet (two by three metres) that stood about one hundred metres from the shallow lake itself. It afforded a clear view of the surrounding hills but was well hidden from view and easily overlooked if you did not know it was nestled in a small clearing surrounded by thick woods. Some say that Kitchener constructed the hut; others say it was already there, originally a stable, which he merely modified to suit his own needs.

Its cramped interior left Kitchener – who was over six feet tall – precious little room to stretch. The wooden plank that served as his bed ran along the short side of the tiny cabin, and in early years, a moose hide served as his mattress. The rough-hewn logs and boards of the walls provided shelving, on which Kitchener kept his treasures – his rifle, papers, his peace pipe, and all sorts of miscellaneous things he made or collected over the years.

Hector MacKenzie approaches Kitchener's hut during a winter visit. (Photo by Dr. Gerry Farrell)

He had constructed his own guitar, a large heavy instrument that sounded remarkably good considering his lack of tools and materials. And he had also inserted glass lenses into wooden frames he shaped himself, which he used as reading glasses until, much later in life, his friends gave him store-bought ones.

Over the years, Kitchener adopted cats that strayed his way. Lloyd Bogle has a photograph of one, grey and long-haired, that slept on the shelf just beside the rifle in the 1970s. When it was no longer there and friends asked about it, Kitchener replied that it had run away because it was "awful scared of strangers" and then he broke into the children's song "The Cat Came Back."

Before the widespread use of snowmobiles in the 1970s and ATVs, or all terrain vehicles, in the 1980s and '90s, the only real paths into the area were those that Kitchener himself had cut. These were not the broad and hard-packed trails they have become in recent years as Gully Lake became a favourite haunt for four-wheelers.

Back then, before Kitchener became well-known and drew visitors almost every weekend to his hideaway, he lived almost entirely on what he was able to hunt, trap, grow and collect, supplementing his diet with a few staples – flour, potatoes, salt – that he obtained at the General Store in Earltown, fourteen kilometres away.

Over the years, he tried to grow a few vegetables himself near his hut, but his crops were not particularly successful in that rocky and shaded garden plot. Some of his nearest neighbours with property bordering on the Gully Lake woodlands say he used to "borrow" vegetables from their gardens, even a chicken or two from their coops. Others say he always left something in return when he did this kind of "trading," taking a few vegetables and leaving an animal pelt or rabbit in exchange.

However, it has to be said that he also annoyed some people by pulling up their potato plants, removing the tubers and then returning the plants to the garden as if to cover up what he had done. With a very few exceptions, there seem to be no hard feelings about this, given the widespread affection and respect for and, failing that, tolerance of Kitchener in the area.

And there *were* people in the area who did little more than tolerate Kitchener. One elderly man says Kitchener was "smart as a fox" when it came to avoiding people to whom he owed money. While others toiled on farms or in sawmills and in the woods day in and day out, year after year to survive those difficult years of the 1940s and '50s, Kitchener would order firewood in to his camp on Jack Gunn's Hill then arrange not to be there when it was unloaded and whenever they went in seeking payment afterwards.

But even his critics sigh and shake their heads when they contemplate how difficult life must have been for him. They recognize that without the support – voluntary or otherwise – of the community, friends and family, Kitchener would have had trouble surviving.

Over the years, friends and well-wishers provided him with bicycles, skis and snowshoes to make the long trek into Earltown for shopping a little less arduous. But in the late 1950s and the '60s, he was still a strong man, and he seems not to have had a great deal of trouble getting about and finding what he needed to survive.

The lake was full of red-bellied trout and, according to one man who used to run across Kitchener up in Gully Lake, he also had a small boat that he would lend to fishermen who went up there.

Melvin MacKay agrees that Kitchener had no trouble providing for himself in those years. "Willard was quite a trout fisherman," says Melvin, with his raspy laugh. "He could catch a trout in the lake but they wouldn't bite for me."

Kitchener had his army issue .303 rifle, and was able to obtain ammunition for it in Earltown, for hunting deer, as well as moose and rabbits. He would smoke and dry the meat, and store it out behind his shack in a lean-to of plastic and spruce bows. At one point, the stove that sat in the middle of the hut was fashioned from the body of an old wringer-washer. He then replaced that with a five-gallon barrel and, much later, a small woodstove that someone had given him or he had found somewhere – but the flue was still a treacherous length of thin aluminium hose for a clothes dryer that poked through the log walls.

Hector MacKenzie had not seen Kitchener in more than twenty years when he first made his way to Gully Lake to renew his acquaintance with him in 1968 or 1969, whichever year it was he got his first snowmobile – he's no longer sure when that was. He says at that time, Kitchener was pretty much independent of the outside world.

"He had plenty of meat and there was plenty of fish in the lake. He also did some trapping. He'd have a few hides to take out, and Murphy at the General Store in Earltown would help him sell the hides. He made axe handles too. He told us one time he could get pretty near a year out of a moose. He would dry the meat."

Hector recalls, with his trademark laugh that must have rocked and ricocheted in Willard's tiny hut at Gully Lake many a time, that Kitchener was generous with these provisions he had laid up to see him through the long and hard winters. "It was pretty hard to turn him down, but pretty hard to accept that moose meat too," he says. "It was pretty unappealing with hair all ground into it."

Robert Clark, who used to see him frequently both in the camp near Earltown and later the one at Gully Lake because of Jessie's regular visits with her son, says even in the summer Kitchener would have a deer strung up that he was using for meat, not concerned that it was rotten.

"But he never got sick," says Hector MacKenzie. "He said that he never even had a cold, not until all those people started coming in from all over to see him." Ruth Smith says Kitchener told her exactly the same thing.

The only entrance to the hut was the south-facing window through which he crawled to get in or out. Those who visited him regularly in the last two decades of his life say he always kept that window locked, placing saw blades across it when he wasn't there, to deter nosy passers-by from intruding.

Some people, individuals who certainly had no romantic illusions about Kitchener and did not count themselves as his friends but who did go up to Gully Lake to fish or hunt, speak of other less savoury things he used to frighten off unwanted visitors. They call his place "very creepy."

"He mounted animal skulls on trees around his hovel," says one man. "And he put reflectors in the eye sockets and if you shone your flashlight on one of those in the night, I tell you it made you run."

In the winter of 1971, Lloyd Bogle began heading up to Gully Lake on his snowmobile with his friend Bobby Matheson, searching for the deserter said to be living like a hermit in the woods there. It took them two Saturdays to find his place, but when they did they found him very friendly.

"He was cutting wood and we helped him cut wood. He took us in and we had a cup of tea, we had our tea with us, and we spent all day there talking to him," says Lloyd. "He made us feel welcome, or else we wouldn't have stayed. And we had a tremendous lot of fun that winter, going back there and cutting wood for him. Playing music, laughing, whatever."

After that, Lloyd forged a friendship with Kitchener that would last till the very end. Lloyd became one of Kitchener's most influential connections with the outside world, his conduit to the media that made him "famous" and to those who would eventually get him social security and then pension money.

Lloyd generally came with a friend or two, usually fellow musicians and lovers of old-time fiddle music. They always brought along a bottle and some tobacco and the mandatory musical instruments to turn a weekend day into a lengthy jam session in the woods. Although they might also bring along some food – sandwiches and other homemade delicacies prepared by their wives – Kitchener often refused to touch this food and if he did, took only tiny amounts. He said he couldn't eat much at a time after all those years of living with so little.

Hector recalls how he and his friends used to take their own dinners in with them. They would offer Kitchener some beans or hotdogs or whatever they had along, and he wouldn't eat one bite. He remembers that his wife once sent some baked biscuits in with Hector and his friends. They were fresh out of the oven, he says, but Kitchener wouldn't even touch them. "Put them there," Kitchener said, pointing to the front step of the house.

Lloyd MacIntosh says that even when Kitchener came out of the woods down to Loganville to visit with him, he rarely accepted anything to eat. The only time he recalls Kitchener sitting down for a cup of tea and a meal was one morning when it was snowing hard and had been all night, and the recluse showed up at the door saying he had been caught by the storm and had frozen his feet.

"He was suspicious of everyone," says Lloyd MacIntosh. "He seemed to like me, probably because I didn't disturb him or ask him questions. But it seemed he thought people might want to poison him."

Lloyd Bogle's wife Helen says the only thing Kitchener did seem to like that she sent with her husband, or took up when she accompanied him to Gully Lake, was her molasses cookies.

But Kitchener didn't have much of a sweet tooth, at least not back in the 1970s and '80s. He lived primarily from the pancakes he made in that hubcap-cum-stovetop lid, using flour, sugar and salt he obtained from the General Store in Earltown, and from wild game he hunted or trapped.

Kitchener enjoying a drink during an afternoon jam session with friends. His winter food supply of smoked and dried eels hang from the rafters of his hut. (Photo by Lloyd Bogle)

Eels were also an important component of his winter diet. These, Kitchener said, he caught in the brooks around the lake, and after smoking and drying them, he dangled hundreds of the small eels head-down from the low ceiling of his hut. Visitors who asked about the eels, how he caught them and what he did with them, sometimes got more than they bargained for. That is, Kitchener would start pulling the little dried fellows down from the low rafters and generously share his winter food supply, giving handfuls of desiccated eels to his visitors to take home and try. They were dandy in stew, he said. You could soak them for a day and then pound them to put in soups, he said, or just fry them up as they were.

"They kept well," says Lloyd Bogle, with a chuckle. "I never ate them but they lasted."

Lloyd says at that time, Kitchener was doing a lot of trapping, mostly muskrat and the odd beaver, otter, mink and fox, and that his friend and fellow musician Bobby Matheson would take those pelts out for him to River John to sell for about two hundred dollars a batch. He also helped sell the axe handles Kitchener crafted.

Kitchener's knowledge of the flora and fauna of his forest home could probably have filled several volumes of nature guides. Some people who visited him say he wrote down everything he observed about the nature around him, filling pages and pages. In this pursuit, he was following in the time-honoured tradition of many a hermit, writer and philosopher down through the millennia. In the 1800s, William Wordsworth, Ralph Waldo Emerson and Henry David Thoreau, for example, all cherished solitude and revered nature and wrote copious amounts about how the two were almost mystically linked; one could only be fully appreciated in the presence of the other.

Kitchener told visitors that he collected wild berries, nuts, mushrooms and wild plants that constituted not just food but also medicines. He was fascinated by and had enormous respect for Native understanding of nature, and often spoke about this to friends, saying Native people were "smarter than the white man in some ways."

He said he particularly liked something he called "wild cucumbers" that he found in the bog. He described this plant as one having a straight stem and a circle of leaves around the top, like a core, with the "cucumber" part underground. He ate that raw, he said, as he did the hazelnuts he collected.

Lloyd Bogle asked him how he managed to learn which plants tasted good or could be used as medicines, without poisoning himself. Kitchener told him that he started out consuming only very tiny amounts at a time, and if there were no adverse effects, he continued to consume that plant in increasing quantities. He seems to have experimented very much the way any scientist would with an unknown food or medicinal plant, except that he used himself as the guinea pig.

Living as he did more with nature than with human beings, Kitchener also developed an extraordinary repertoire of animal calls, and he spent a fair amount of his time in the woods learning to commune with the moose, squirrels and birds – owls, ravens, blue jays – with which he shared the forest. He could also perform a very impressive yodel, worthy not just of Gully Lake but the Bavarian Alps. He said he yodelled to cheer himself up.

Apart from the hut near Gully Lake that became his home base in the late 1960s, over the years Kitchener seems to have roamed widely and set up other makeshift camps all over the area. He may have retired to these when the traffic through his formerly remote stomping grounds became a little heavy as more ATV and snowmobile trails were established around the lake, and also as more and more people were lured to the area to meet this famous "hermit."

The remains of one of these camping spots can still be seen near an area known as Juniper Meadow, about three hundred metres north of the site of the burned-out hut that was his home from the 1960s onwards. Against a large boulder, there are remnants of a lean-to he erected many years earlier. Around the rock are still scattered half a dozen grocery bags full of old clothing – woollen hats, work pants, shirts – and a few discarded rusted-out utensils, kettles and pans. Kitchener told David Smith that he set up this camp to sit out a bout of snow-blindness he suffered while on a winter hunt.

Many of those who knew him figure he probably had a whole network of camping spots in the hills around Gully Lake, places he stayed while setting or checking traplines or just because he liked to wander in the woods.

David says that Kitchener claimed to have seen wolverines and cougars, both of which, he says, "are not supposed to live in the area." But David is a bit sceptical of government officials with their expertise on which animals can – or cannot – be found around Gully Lake. He says he saw a black cougar at the tip of the lake, another species that is officially unknown in Nova Scotia, and that when he reported his sighting, officials dismissed it out of hand.

David also says that Kitchener saw snakes in the area that "aren't supposed to be there," including a red and black one that bit him, inducing fever and aches for a month afterwards. And David has seen a snake that resembles a water moccasin in the stream that runs down from Gully Lake to Loganville, passing through the Smith farm.

Kitchener was once quoted as saying he had chosen the area because it was "as far as you could go in before you started coming out the other side." Of course, he had lived and trekked in that part of the province bordering Pictou and Colchester Countries since his youth.

Tatamagouche teacher, writer and inveterate runner-cum-explorer Norris Whiston, who studied old maps and geological surveys of the area around Gully Lake, says he "ran the place" many times. He wrote a delightful short story about his meetings with Kitchener which appeared in a running newsletter. Norris once gave Kitchener a topographical map, thinking the old man might be curious about how the locations that he knew so intimately might be drawn and appear on paper. He may well have been.

Topographical maps of Gully Lake and environs show that the highest point of land in the area is to the southeast of the lake itself, a ridge of high land that appears on the map shaped just like a cat's head with the two ears clearly delineated. David Smith says that Kitchener knew all about that topographical feature and even called it the "Cat's Head." Together, they spent a good deal of time up on that high ridge trapping and hunting. David is convinced that his friend had another camp up there, close to the tip of one of the formations that on a map resembled cat's ears.

Kitchener also claimed that he prospected for gold in Gully Lake, and after his death, rumours abounded in the area that perhaps he had amassed great wealth and hidden it somewhere in those hills. There was talk about how much he might have inherited from his mother when she passed away in 1980, and some sources say that she bequeathed him a piece of land in Loch Broom that he sold for $2,500 according to some, $4,500 according to others, a sum he is believed to have deposited in the recently closed bank in River John. Others speak about cheques he might have collected from his trapping and never cashed. And some people also allude to the mysterious crash of a military plane carrying troops with their paycheques during World War II near Dalhousie in the hills of northern Nova Scotia and what might have been scavenged from that crash site. As always, the void created by a shortage of verifiable facts and figures rapidly fills with fantastic myths and wild – but intriguing – speculation.

Certainly, though, there *is* gold in those hills. Mineral inventory studies show deposits of the economically important association of iron-oxide-copper-gold and there are existing mineral rights in the area of Gully Lake in the hands of prospectors and mining companies. Kitchener would have been aware over the years that mineral companies were prospecting a good deal around Gully Lake. But Lloyd Bogle, for one, was not convinced that Kitchener's own prospecting had amounted to much, even if his extensive knowledge of the area might have included a good idea of where gold could be found and an interest in what minerals or gems might be buried in the ground he walked over.

Lillie Stewart, who got to know Kitchener in the 1980s, says that during one visit he gave her a handful of pebbles he had collected, asking if she thought they might be valuable. She had them identified by her nephew's son, a geologist, who said they had no monetary value at all. When she went back to see Kitchener, she showed him the scientific names for the various pebbles, written on a geological publication signed for him by her nephew's son. She wanted Kitchener to know that she had taken his curiosity about the stones seriously. He replied that he thought the scientific information was "interesting" and then offered the pebbles to her. But she declined, saying he had gone to the work of collecting them and he should add them to his collection, now that he knew what they were.

During the last decade of Kitchener's life, a debate raged in northern Nova Scotia about what should become of the 4,600 hectares of Crown land around Gully Lake, 3,800 of which remained in a relatively natural condition. Conservation groups, the Nova Scotia Public Lands Coalition and the Ecology Action Centre, had lobbied long and hard to have it turned into a protected wilderness area, of which there were none in Colchester and Pictou Counties. Gully Lake serves as an important watershed for River John, flowing northwards to the Northumberland Strait, and for the Salmon River, flowing southwest towards the Minas Basin. ATV and snowmobile clubs, as well as hunting and fishing associations, seemed to endorse government action that would protect the area from clearcutting and mining, but some expressed concerned about the level of freedom they would have to use the area for recreation were it all designated as protected wilderness. And all the while, powerful industrial interests were lobbying the provincial and municipal governments to keep the area open for business – mining and logging. Parts of the Gully Lake area were already covered by leases to J.D. Irving Ltd. and one to the Swedish multinational Stora Enso for softwood to feed their pulp mills. In 2003 and 2004, gold prospectors representing mining concerns were still making presentations to municipal counsellors, clearly hoping to convince them to apply pressure on the provincial government to ensure the area would be available for gold and other ore extraction, which would not be possible in a protected wilderness area.

In addition to all the buried riches and tree resources around Gully Lake, Kitchener also spoke about an Indian burial near the Cat's Head, and David Smith believes that he retreated to a camp up there when he wanted to disappear.

But Kitchener didn't need any remote camps or hideouts to keep clear of people when he didn't want to see them, or be seen by them. He might lie quietly in dense shrubs or grass if groups of strangers passed, or quietly slip out of his cabin and head off into the deep woods behind it. When he didn't want to be found, no one could find him.

"I asked him one time why people wouldn't find him when they went in," says Ruth Smith. "'Ah,' he said, 'I could smell a rat a mile away.'"

Hector MacKenzie, who went up to Gully Lake with many of his friends from around Salt Springs to visit Kitchener and help cut firewood to see him through the long and cold winters, recalls that there were times he either wouldn't be there when they arrived, or else he might be hiding.

"If I hollered for him, I'd call out, 'Hey Kitsi,' and sure enough way back in the hills he'd answer and we'd wait around, he'd come back, wherever he was, just out walking around."

"But he didn't want us to cut trees right around his cabin. He'd have trees marked back a ways," says Hector. "And one day we were there cutting wood. Billy Johnson's mother came along with us, and she set in the cabin while we were working and during the time we were working, she knit him a pair of mittens. And that night we had a good big pile of wood not far from the cabin. We had it piled up and he crawled up on the pile of wood and he put his head back and he crowed just like a rooster, he was so happy, seeing the wood."

"One time there was a bunch of us and maybe he wasn't sure who it was. But he had been walking in the snow and we followed his tracks . . . but the tracks kind of came to an end and we looked to the right and he was tucked in behind a tree," says Hector with a big laugh. "And we had to encourage him to come out. I'd say, 'Come out of there, you old bugger' and he would come out. But those was the days he was very sceptical about who was visiting him."

Chapter 8
Snow baths and sun worship

Lloyd Bogle says that just as he could make himself physically scarce when he didn't want to be found, when Kitchener didn't want to talk about something, that was the end of it; there was no point trying to pursue the subject. The list of subjects he considered taboo was long – his family, his upbringing, his decision to desert, his move back into the woods, his age, why he refused to sign papers, his feelings – just about any why, when or where question at all.

Sometimes he just wouldn't answer, says Lloyd. Sometimes he would change the subject altogether, use a non sequitur to put an end to a line of questioning or conversation he didn't like. And sometimes he would answer a question – a direct question about his age or how long he had been living in his Gully Lake hut, for example – with the question, "What would Perry Como say?"

When Lloyd confessed to not being sure what exactly Perry Como would say, Kitchener replied, "Perry Como, he was a singer. He had glasses and the reason he wore them was that one day he was walking along the street and his eyes got kind of fuzzy, you know. So he went to an eye doctor, to examine him, and the doctor said, 'How are you today?' and Como said, 'None of your beezness.'"

And the laughter would fill the afternoon.

"I don't know how he knew about Perry Como, but he did," says Lloyd. "I'd ask him a question and he would turn it back on me, and say, 'None of yer beezness,' just like Perry Como. He was his own man." The memories still make Lloyd laugh long and hard.

But there were subjects that Kitchener did love to talk about, in between old-time fiddle classics and tunes he composed himself. Science and philosophy and the Bible were subjects he often raised on his own, tossing out questions to his visitors to find out what their thinking was on a topic or issue that seemed very far removed from Kitchener's reclusive life in the wilderness.

His book collection deeply impressed many visitors who found it incongruous that a man living alone in the woods without electricity, telephone, running water or even a well, in a dank and dark hut, would be such a voracious reader of anything he could get his hands on.

He stacked the books right underneath the window he used as a door, right on the packed mud that was his floor. He did much of his reading by the light this window afforded, or seated just outside. At night he used kerosene lamps and candles, at least when he had the kerosene and the candles on hand. When he had the batteries to power them, in later years he also used flashlights.

The credit for Kitchener's collection of books goes largely to Marilyn MacWah, a retired library assistant who for twenty-six years worked in the bookmobile for the Truro Regional Library. One of her monthly stops was Earltown, or more specifically, Murphy Stonehouse's General Store, which is how she became Kitchener's lifeline to the literary world.

"I think I heard from Murphy that Kitchener was a reader," says Marilyn. "Kitchener would leave a little written note of what books he wanted."

"One year he would like science fiction; the next year he would want books about forests or animals, the next year classics," she says.

She remembers that he liked books by Charles Dickens, ghost stories, westerns, and works about nature.

"I couldn't take the books off the shelves as I would for a regular loan," she says. "They would come back tattered and pretty smelly. So I had to get discards. Sometimes I was able to get the books discarded so I could just leave them with him. Or, if they were still too new for the library to discard, I would go down to the secondhand bookstore in Truro, and pay for them myself."

Marilyn recalls that one of the books Kitchener had requested, which she had to buy from the secondhand bookstore, was *Alice in Wonderland*.

She regrets enormously that she has lost all the handwritten notes from Kitchener, but is grateful that she does have memories of a single visit in to see him in 1996, on the urging of Murphy Stonehouse.

"It was on my wish list of things I wanted to do before I died," she says. "So on November 11, 1996, I was passing through Earltown and Murphy said that was the day. We walked through the woods, a long way, and when we got there he was reading a book. Murphy told him that I was the woman who had brought him all the books, and he said, 'Thank you, I have quite a collection of books.'"

Marilyn says she read him as a very quick-witted person, a little shy, and that it was Murphy who kept the conversation going. "When they had the eightieth birthday party for him, I didn't get in," she says. "What I had heard was that he was a very private man, a woodsy gentleman who wanted to be left alone. He was one of a kind."

Lloyd's sister, Edie Bogle, was one of many who went in to see Kitchener and was deeply impressed by his curiosity and wide interests. Edie, a nurse who has lived in Michigan for nearly forty years but who comes home to Nova Scotia each summer, says that the trip in to see Kitchener in 1994 was one of the greatest experiences of her life.

She says she kept a low profile, didn't approach Kitchener or try to initiate any conversations that might put him off. Rather, she crawled quietly into his little house and had an awed look at the dark, cramped quarters that had been his home for all those years, at the plank of wood spread with spruce bows, a moose skin and a sleeping bag that constituted his bedding.

When she emerged from the hut, Kitchener approached her, and asked her if she knew anything about Aristotle. "And I'm looking at him," she says, "way back in the woods outside of Earltown, at this gentleman talking to me about . . . Aristotle. We had a little conversation about that. Then he asked me about Galileo. He had been looking at the heavens and at all those books. And I thought, 'This man is so intelligent. And so intuitive. And very tuned into nature.' And we talked about that, and then he said, 'What do you know about the theory of evolution, Darwin's theory of evolution?' And I'm thinking, 'No person would believe this.' So I had a long, long conversation with him." She told him a little about the Galapagos Islands, where Darwin had studied the fauna and flora and refined his work on the origin of the species, about which Kitchener said he hadn't heard and in which he appeared to be very interested.

"And then I asked him if he finds the time long," Edie says. "'No,' he said to me, 'I don't find the time long.'"

Lloyd Bogle says he's not sure that Kitchener actually read *all* those books that were stacked up under the window of his hut, but he is sure that his friend was a very intelligent man with a great deal of curiosity and intellectual capacity.

Kitchener's knowledge of the outside world seems to have been limited to what he may have heard on his irregular forays out to Earltown to the General Store, a meeting place for people and ideas in the area, to what he heard on a small radio that worked only on those rare occasions that he had batteries to power it, and to what he could glean from the books, magazines and newspapers that friends brought in. He asked far more questions than he answered, at least on the audio cassettes that captured many hours of conversations Lloyd and his friends had with Kitchener. He also seemed averse to making judgments on anything or anyone, and certainly did not gossip or even speak about people he knew, so that few were aware of just how many people he did know in later life. Although he didn't always have his facts straight, he seemed very tolerant of beliefs and customs that were certainly not the prevailing cultural norm in northern Nova Scotia.

During an afternoon of music and conversation recorded by Lloyd Bogle in March, 1982, Kitchener said, "Meat is good for a fella. Jews don't eat meat at all. Some people won't eat pork, and in Africa and India some people won't eat cattle either. That's their way. I wouldn't like to interfere with anyone."

After some equivocal murmurs from Lloyd and his friend Dave Buckler, an accomplished violinist, guitar and banjo player who had gone in that day, Kitchener continued. "I wouldn't like to be up in front of a bunch of people and tell them what to do," he said. "Like them preachers."

When Dave Buckler told him a little about his own life as a radio operator for Transport Canada, which had taken him to Toronto and to Goose Bay in Labrador before bringing him back to Nova Scotia, Kitchener pondered for a moment before responding.

"Goose Bay," he said. "Is that where that big rock is, a hundred miles high and a hundred miles wide? Did you ever hear tell of that rock? I read in a book that there is a rock in the north, one hundred miles high and wide. Wouldn't it have blocked out the sun?"

Dave diplomatically explained that the sun was millions of miles away and that it would not be completely blocked out by such a rock, even if it existed. He went on to speak of the clouds of volcanic dust emitted by the eruption of Mount St. Helen in 1980, which were indeed blocking out some of the sun's rays when this conversation took place in 1982. Dave said that this dust cloud was being studied and measured by laser beams. Kitchener was intrigued.

"I'm very interested in that stuff," he said. "I seen a lot of strange things, and I can't explain why it happens."

At one point that afternoon, Lloyd Bogle exclaimed that the lid of the stove had fallen in. After finding his flashlight in the gloom of the interior, Lloyd reached inside the stove to retrieve the lid, asking, "What'd you make this stove out of, Kitchener? Cement?"

"A flying saucer," replied Kitchener.

The lid that Lloyd retrieved was, in fact, the old Chevrolet hubcap that Kitchener used as a stove lid, frying pan, and plate.

Over the many years Kitchener spent on his own with animals and birds for company, surrounded by trees and the lake, and under star-filled heavens undimmed by urban smog and light pollution, he had few of the modern distractions and easy entertainment to which many of us resort in the evenings and on weekends to pass the time. Perhaps partly because of this, he developed an insatiable thirst for knowledge and understanding of some of the greater puzzles of the universe.

Kitchener had the active and unspoiled imagination of a child who has never been told to colour within the lines or to stop asking so many questions, a mind unfettered by the reality-checks that constrain most North American adult thought processes today. Most people on this continent are constantly on the run, juggling commitments, struggling to pay the bills and keep up with ever-more-complex technologies. We are expected to digest far too much information, and bow to pressure to conform and consume. We barely have time to think, let alone to step back and savour the mysteries of life – big or small.

Kitchener's life and mind were not strapped onto the narrow rails of the crazy roller coaster that is modern life. He felt no obligation to keep up any appearances whatsoever, unless it were to perform later on in the role cast for him by the world as an eccentric and almost saintly hermit. Then, it was as if he offered a counter to the avarice and vanity that increasingly shape our own pop culture – as shown on "reality television." It wasn't so much that he rejected the material culture of our modern world. It's just that he had never grown used to it. He was the original Survivor. And his thoughts flitted from one thing to another, much like the birds he loved so much moved – apparently erratically – from one tree to another.

Out of the blue on that March afternoon in the company of Lloyd Bogle and Dave Buckler, after a prolonged silence Kitchener suddenly blurted out, "I read in a book that an Englishman's castle is his own home. He can do what he pleases, but in a public building they can arrest him."

"That applies to any man," Dave Buckler replied.

"You can do anything you please in your own home," Kitchener said then. "You can scream, you can yell, you can kick the roof off. And there's no one can do a thing about it."

"Can you figure that out?" was a question that Kitchener often attached to the end of his musings. "There's a lot of stuff in the books," he would say. "I'm trying to figure it out."

One has the impression that he felt obliged to try to entertain his visitors, or if the mood struck him, to amuse them with his antics or his large repertoire of jokes. Many of these seemed to have come from the pages of *Reader's Digest* or old Jack Benny radio shows from the 1930s, '40s and '50s, which he may have heard before his self-imposed exile in the woods.

One of the things he loved to do to amuse his visitors – and to stimulate his own mind, he said – was to stand on his head, which he could do for long periods of time. After a few drinks and if he seemed to be enjoying his visitors, he might challenge them to try standing on their heads, which some would try valiantly to do, usually without great success. Kitchener would push them gently aside and show them how it was done. Or without warning, he might just start calling to the crows when he felt the urge, and tip himself onto his head and stay there, legs in the air, for a few minutes.

Hector MacKenzie recalls that Kitchener used to say the whole world was "going kinda upside-down," and that he wanted to see if it was still that way when he was standing on his head.

During the visit in March, 1982, when Lloyd asked him if he was going to stand on his head today, Kitchener said, "Hail Caesar." Asked why he said that, he replied, "The book says to say it, so I say it, you know, just for scientific curiosity. No harm to anyone?"

"No," said Lloyd. "You're not doing anybody any harm."

And Kitchener responded, "I want to do people good if I can. I'm as harmless as I can be."

He said he had read about the beneficial effects of yoga, and he also took snow baths. He maintained that these were recommended by the Bible that told the faithful to "wash thyself in the treasure of snow." He said he heated himself up to one degree shy of the boiling point, and then ran out to jump in the snow.

"You just roll over and rub the snow over you until you turn blue," Kitchener said. "Then you run back in and get warmed up." And you had to be "right stripped naked" for such a bath.

"The first time I done it, I heard someone groan, and it was me!" he said. "I didn't know I was doing it. I think I was connecting there to the other side. After that, I seemed to feel better."

He said that he took a snow bath each time there was a good snow. But you had to know how to do it correctly.

"Sometimes I go in ice cold water like the Indians do," he said. "That's worse because you break the ice to get into it. That's dangerous. I talked to another fella and he said he tried it and it darned near killed him. And I seen a dog jump in cold water in the winter; it went under the ice and then come out. Never seen a dog run that fast."

He explained that his snow bath was the same thing as the sauna of the Swedish and Native people who heated themselves up in their log cabins or tents before jumping in ice water.

"I tried it because they say in the book that if God is for you, He can also be against you. God is all powerful. I read the Bible quite a lot and try and understand it, but I can't understand it. It seems to be confused. It says in the book that a house that is divided cannot stand and I think myself that the world should become united in one belief. There are so many mixtures of beliefs now. What do you think?" Kitchener asked Lloyd and Dave. Before they could search for an answer, Kitchener suddenly began cawing like a crow.

In October 1982, Lloyd Bogle was visiting with another group of friends and musicians, when Kitchener decided to divulge the details of the morning ritual he said he performed every day.

"You just face the sun and rise with the sun and there's supposed to be power in the air, wisdom and power. Some of these people they're very religious, whatever you want to call it, scientific, and they're going through the ceremony. There are brainwaves, part of your brain goes into the atmosphere, and you go through the motions and you absorb that."

Lloyd, sounding a little perplexed, asked him if he got the power from the sun.

"Well, you can, but you get the power, the electricity from the air, you absorb that," Kitchener replied. "You have to be very faithful and do it every morning. Even if it's cloudy, there is still a sunrise just the same. The sun is still there. I always rise before that, just at the break of dawn. You absorb that in your system."

"I'm what you call a sun worshipper," he said. "I bow to the sun. I think the Japanese are like that. I don't know if they go through the same ceremony I do or not. Anyway, I been going to churches, or I heard about them but there doesn't seem to be nothing in them."

During a break in the music that October day, when asked what he would like to do most if he had his choice, Kitchener said, "Oh, I think I'd like to get a good education."

Then he went on to show the depths of his mistrust of those in authority, a latent and simmering paranoia that revealed itself often in his discussions with friends and an oft-repeated claim that songs and stories he had written had somehow been stolen and were being used by others to make money.

"These people that gave us an education here, they don't tell you everything," Kitchener said. "There's a lot of stuff that people don't know. I'd like to go to school. I'd like to learn some of this stuff."

"Math and science?" inquired Lloyd.

"Yeah, I'd like to know true stories. You take the Bible; some say it's a false Bible. I don't know if that's true or not. Anyway, I read that somewhere there is a true Bible, handed down direct from Jesus. They have it there in their archives, the true Bible."

"If you had all the money you wanted, what would you do?" asked Lloyd.

"I think I'd like to go some place where everyone is free," Kitchener replied. "Where everyone is treated the same. Wouldn't you?"

"Are you happy the way you are? You have a certain amount of peace of mind, don't you, Kitchener?" Lloyd asked.

"I know this is not the real life," answered the ever-enigmatic Kitchener.

"But you do have a sense of peace of mind?" Lloyd persisted.

"Oh, I suppose," he replied. "Aim in life is the only fortune worth finding."

At first glance, that seems a strange statement to come from Kitchener, but perhaps not. Perhaps his aim was fairly straightforward: to survive in the wilderness and to learn whatever he could whenever the opportunity presented itself. If that is indeed the case, then some might say he had found his fortune.

Chapter 9
Fiddler in the woods

Music seems to have been Kitchener's greatest passion. This is not particularly surprising for a man whose entire immediate family all played instruments and whose father's talents on the violin earned him the name Fiddle Foot. He was also a product of his times, growing up in northern Nova Scotia where old-time fiddle music continues to be the most powerful social adhesive and a common language linking generations.

For quite a few years, between the 1950s when he would still show up to play at dances and the 1980s when musicians began to flock to Gully Lake to play with him almost every weekend, he had to make his own music – and his own guitar, for which he cut and shaped the wood for the body. Local legend has it that he descended to Earltown to a pasture to pluck hair from horses' tails to make the strings in those years before he could get most of what he needed from Murphy's General Store or from visiting friends and benefactors.

His many friends and acquaintances, at least those interviewed for this book, certainly do not all agree about Kitchener: on what kind of man he was; how much of a hermit he really was; how much of what he said to visitors was sincere and how much of it was mischievous pulling of people's legs; how happy he was living on his own in the woods; or why he lived as he did. But there *is* one thing every single one of those people did agree on – and that was the importance of music in his life.

The thing for which he is best remembered as a young man in Earltown was his guitar and fiddle playing at local dances. His cousin Shirley Sutherland Miller has no recollection of him speaking when she and her parents visited the MacDonald family home in Pictou, but she clearly remembers his aptitude for the violin, when he was summoned by his father to accompany him.

Few people who visited with him in the last three decades of his life went without an arsenal of musical instruments, sometimes enough for a complete band, replete with keyboard. The list of artists who went up is impressive. Lloyd Bogle, himself a guitarist and aficionado of old-time fiddle music, took up many accomplished musicians over the years. From Pictou, Darryl Gamble, Lloyd's cousin, also went up with groups of well-known musicians – sometimes also with their musical teenagers – and some of these afternoon jamborees at Gully Lake were captured on home videos. In one, belonging to Harold Ferguson in Pictou, Kitchener plays along with the gang in a rousing rendition of "When The Saints Go Marching In," and as the chorus ends, Kitchener says, "One of these days they will."

Harold Ferguson was so impressed by Kitchener's music and his story that he took several precious days off from running his business in Pictou and drove to the Windsor Exhibition in Hants County, Nova Scotia, where the CBC-TV crew from Wayne Rostad's *On the Road Again* were filming. He offered the producers the video of Kitchener and friends playing outside his Gully Lake hut, and pitched the story of the remarkable "Hermit" – in vain. Nothing ever came of his efforts and to this day, Harold says he is dismayed that they passed over a story he feels would have greatly impressed Canadian viewers for others in northern Nova Scotia that he feels had no merit whatsoever.

An afternoon jam session at Gully Lake in April 2002 with Kitchener (centre) on guitar, Frank Hart (far left), Harry Brooks (kneeling on left), John Meir on accordian (second from right) and Dave Gunning (far right). (Photo by Hector MacKenzie)

Hector MacKenzie also accompanied many musicians to Gully Lake over the years, including the young East Coast Music Award-winning songwriter and singer from Pictou, Dave Gunning. Together John Meir of Pictou's deCoste Centre and Dave co-wrote a beautiful song dedicated to Kitchener, "Let Him Be" for his 2004 CD *Two-bit World*.

Dave says he had been reluctant to go in and see Kitchener, simply because he figured the old man would "not have been living out there if he wanted a lot of visitors." But eventually, in April 2002, he did go in, joining Hector MacKenzie, John Meir, and a few other musicians who turned Kitchener's front step into a veritable bandstand in the woods.

Dave was greatly impressed by Kitchener's humility. "He wouldn't bring out his old guitar," he says. "He seemed embarrassed by it and told us it was in rough shape." When Kitchener did play on a guitar borrowed from one of the visitors, Dave was struck by the unusual chording of the ballads he played. He says the melodies and chords sounded almost Middle Eastern, and the lyrics of the songs Kitchener composed were intense.

"He seemed inspired; he seemed to go someplace else and open up his soul more when he was singing," says Dave. "But talking to him, he was pretty quiet. He almost seemed painfully humble. He seemed to think, 'I'm a zero out of ten. Why am I important to you?' He had a great humility." And Dave suggests the world might just be a better place if we all considered ourselves – as Kitchener did – zeroes out of ten.

While his fiddling skills were definitely rusty by the 1980s and '90s, as he had lived many years without access to a violin, Kitchener was still able to make his way through many an old-time favourite – highland Scottish hornpipe reels, country songs by Hank Williams, Hank Snow, Marty Robbins, Merle Haggard, Johnny Cash, and Wilf Carter (also known as Montana Slim). He was very fond of a song by country music legend Marvin Rainwater, about chasing a bluebird. But he did say one afternoon, "I like the Scotch pretty good. I think it's the best music in the world." And on another occasion he said, "I think music is the best thing in the world; it's good for the soul."

He said he had tried to play every song in a book of a thousand fiddle tunes, but mastered only a few of them. He said he wished he could write down notes because often he forgot or got confused trying to play his own songs. He claimed to have composed one hundred and fifty of his own songs, but said to Lloyd Bogle with a laugh, "I wouldn't want to play them all on one day for you. I don't want to hog the show."

On the various audio cassettes Lloyd recorded over the years, and on the video recordings made by others who went up to play music with him, Kitchener appears to have been much more at ease on the guitar, probably because of the endless hours he must have spent strumming away on the guitar he made himself. He liked to show off with Spanish rhythms and chords and said that he had once studied opera.

He could imitate a Mexican, a woman from the southern U.S., even an accent that sounded like it might have been French. Sometimes he would just start speaking in an unintelligible language that appeared to be all his own.

"Kamate sika, sa, kada, kamato, siko, saga . . . kama kita," is as close as I can come to transcribing the words he would start to utter, out of the blue, while Lloyd and his musical friends were there and the tape was running.

Lloyd asked him what that meant. And Kitchener just repeated the long sentence, before saying in English, and in a very dramatic doomsday voice, "Beware the wrath of the righteous man; it is like lightning. It can destroy a whole city."

Kitchener's first cousin, Shirley, asked him about that language. "He did that little thing he always did with his hand on his chin," she says. "And then he said to me, 'That was three languages, Shirley.'" He mentioned French, Spanish and Latin. But it wasn't any of those, so Shirley decided to call it the "Willard language."

If you told him something was good, says Shirley, he might answer you by saying, "Not bad for a holy ghost." She says it is a shame that no one ever wrote down and catalogued his many sayings, because he had an encyclopaedia of them in his head.

Two songs he composed himself he played frequently for Lloyd Bogle. He said he wrote the music for them, but found the words in books. Both are disturbing songs with dark and unsettling lyrics with a host of different accents and characters, whose voices Kitchener adopted like a born actor.

"I do impersonation, you know, take a different voice," he said to Lloyd. "I get an ordinary story in a magazine, and I put the guitar in and the voices and that's the way it come out."

One of the songs was about Barney, with remarkable lyrics that changed from one performance to another and which Kitchener says he found in a cowboy book. Although not all is audible on the tape, the song is remarkable not so much for its music as for the incredible vocal agility Kitchener displays switching accents and voices throughout.

Introduced with some strident strumming, Kitchener chants in a deep southern twang, "Gonna get someone to dance, gonna get someone to read poems, someone to splash paint like a poet on the dancers, that's about it . . ." The song, half-sung and half-spoken, seems to be a running dialogue between a man, Barney, and his wife, Harriet. The story seems to be set in a kitchen, with Kitchener perfectly taking on the voice of the woman and the man, throughout, as they talk about chores and rain and the sun appearing, along with a woman called Beth. Like many a poem or song, there seems to be some deep meaning there but it would be hard to say exactly what it is.

The second of the songs was about an earthquake, with lyrics that vary from one recording to another on Lloyd's audiotapes. But on one afternoon, this is what he sang: "One night we was standing looking at the ground then something humping round, a hound, made a sound that wasn't round, everybody run, there's a ghost in the sky. Then there came an earthquake that shook things up quite a bit, a crack in the earth forty thousand miles long had everybody running. That monster came out of the crack grew taller and taller. Everybody run. When do you want the end of the earth to come? They said, 'Next month.' Everybody run, they run and they run."

And in an eerie falsetto the dramatic finale to the song: "There's a ghost in the sky and the end of the world is nigh."

On each occasion that Lloyd and his friends showed up with a small cassette player to record the music and conversations during their visit, Kitchener displayed renewed suspicion about their intentions. He wanted to know what they were planning to do with the tape and whether they were going to sell it and make money from it.

In 1982, he said, "I suspect that my music and voice was already used in productions but I got nothing. This world now, the way it is, there's a lot of crooked people. I used to sing opera and I suspect that my voice was used dubbing in the soundtrack, but I suppose I can't do anything about it. The world is crooked."

Speaking to Lloyd he said, "I can write, my dear boy, I wrote a story. I been cheated all my life. I wrote a story about old cars and I sent it in to *Reader's Digest*, and they said they were going to hold it for a year, let me know, and I noticed parts of it in another magazine and I never got one bloody cent. Nothing."

"My ideas have been used," he said. "I'm just a slave. I found that out a few years ago and it made me kinda mad."

He also claimed that he was the inventor of the transistor radio and the power saw – that his ideas had been stolen and he had never received the recognition and remuneration he deserved.

How much of this did Kitchener really believe? Should we take all these comments completely seriously and literally, or as evidence that Kitchener suffered from mild paranoia and delusion? No, says Hector MacKenzie, with a laugh. In his view, Kitchener loved to pull people's legs. He could ham it up in song, adopting any voice and accent he needed; he could ham it up in front of the cameras and in front of those who listened to him with rapt attention, sometimes with something approaching the reverence of a disciple before a spiritual leader. Hector thinks Kitchener was a terrible tease, full of mischief, and it would be misleading to take at face value all that he said to those who entered his private world there at Gully Lake. So it was often impossible to tell what he did and didn't believe, when he was teasing and when he wasn't, or when he was distracting his guests from posing personal questions by inserting red herring comments into the discussions.

Hector says he certainly couldn't claim to really understand Kitchener and he's not sure anyone really could. "Sometimes in conversation you'd be talking about one thing and making a connection with him and the next minute he'd be off onto something else," he says. "He would tell you about seeing these flying saucers, he'd get going on that. Sometimes he'd be telling you this stuff and you'd wonder if he wasn't trying to figure out if people was gullible enough to swallow what he was saying."

And when Kitchener said to people that he hated living in the woods, that he wouldn't wish his life on anyone, was that the truth?

"No," says Hector. "He told them a lot of that stuff to get rid of them."

Ruth Smith also figures much of what Kitchener said to strangers may have just been his own subtle way of telling them — in the teasing but polite way of gentlemen of his generation — to go away and leave him alone.

I have looked at Willard Kitchener MacDonald posthumously and only with the hindsight afforded by the tales his friends and acquaintances tell, the television and newspaper reports, and many hours of audio and video tape recorded over the years. And it does look to me as if he derived a good deal of pleasure from the role he was playing — when he was in the mood — for his increasingly large audience. Certainly, he was far too intelligent and wary to allow himself to be pushed into doing something he didn't want to do or into doing anything that was not on his own terms. So he may not have sought the notoriety or the attention or his growing "fame," but if he had wanted to, he certainly could have avoided it simply by refusing to be interviewed or recorded or even being found by all those visitors. There is no evidence at all that he suffered from scoptophobia, the term for an abnormal and persistent fear of being seen or stared at. Otherwise, surely he would have gone on the run when those television lenses were aimed at him, rather than facing them the way he did, sometimes with alacrity.

I may be wrong, but I do have the sneaking feeling that part of him came to enjoy the power he had to dazzle his visitors with enigmatic comments. He would come up with all sorts of disconnected ideas and names that he had collected from books and stored in the high-walled, secret archives of his mind. Then he would drop them into a conversation like pebbles he might toss into the middle of a placid Gully Lake — and sit back and amuse himself by watching the ripples form and spread.

Chapter 10
Proud, stubborn and ... healthy

One of the questions many people asked themselves – and also asked Kitchener – was how he managed to survive and stay healthy in his tiny hut through the long, dark, cold and snowy winters atop that hill in northern Nova Scotia. Most Canadians in the latter half of the twentieth century and the early years of the third millennium have become accustomed to modern medical care in pristine hospitals and doctors' offices. As a result, we find it almost impossible to imagine making it through even a year – let alone a lifetime – without visiting a doctor or a dentist, a hospital or a pharmacy.

Not that "modern medicine" as we know it is the only way to approach health care. Long before the age of modern Western medicine and the profitable pharmaceutical industry that drives it, China had developed highly sophisticated approaches to medical care that have proven to be extremely effective, even if it has taken the rather overbearing West a long time to admit it. In fact, all human societies through the ages have had their expert medical practitioners, to whom people could turn when their bodies or minds ailed, when they succumbed to fever and pain caused by viruses, bacteria, stress, psychosomatic conditions (including curses and spells cast on them) or just the body's own immune system going a little awry.

Native peoples in Canada had highly sophisticated herbal and spiritual remedies and rituals to heal. Traditional societies the world over still rely mainly on cures, many from medicinal plants, administered by highly skilled practitioners whose knowledge has been bequeathed to them by many generations of specialists. In many countries in Africa, for example, up to eighty percent of the population still rely almost entirely on herbal medicine and their own traditional doctors to heal them. They trust Western medical practitioners only for diagnoses. Today many people in North America are turning to alternative medicine, visiting holistic doctors and seeking massage therapists, acupuncturists and herbal treatments.

But Willard Kitchener MacDonald had none of the above – no doctor, no hospital, no village healer, not even a village to fall back on when his health failed him. When he moved into the woods, he did not have the same range of knowledge of plants and plant medicines that an indigenous person would have had in years past. He may indeed have known some of the remedies our grandmothers and great-grandmothers knew and used, often successfully, which he might have picked up as a child. But the fact remains, he was still very much on his own in those woods, a long trek on foot or on snowshoe, a long bicycle ride or a long journey on skis from the nearest doctor's office or hospital in Tatamagouche or Truro. If, that is, he ever chose to see a modern medical doctor – which he did not. He shunned modern medicine and he shunned attempts by his friends to look out for his health. He said there was no need for pills, advising visitors who complained of pain *not* to pop aspirin.

And yet, remarkably, he seems to have had few serious health problems, at least none to which he admitted and none of which his friends were aware. As Ruth Smith says, he claimed he never even had a cold until people began to visit him and bring their viruses with them.

As a nurse, Edie Bogle had a particular interest in how a man who lived on his own – without access to modern medicine and no inclination to take any even if he had, with only the bare minimum to eat and nothing most people in North America assumed were necessities for life – could remain healthy. Indeed, one of the questions she wanted to answer when she went in to visit him in 1994 with her brother Lloyd, was whether he really was healthy.

Her overriding impression when she first laid eyes on him is that he was. First, she says, he was "as agile as a cat" when he moved through the woods, silently and nimbly making his way over the boulders in the narrow paths around his cabin. "He was lean," she says, "very, very lean. Not a bit of fat on him."

Edie had taken her stethoscope and blood pressure gauge and cuff with her, hoping to have the chance to use these to check his vital signs. When she pulled them out, however, Kitchener "took off," heading around the corner of his hut. So instead, she took the blood pressure of her brother, Lloyd. When she noticed Kitchener watching from his hiding place, she invited him to come and hold the gauge, which he did, while she explained what it was measuring. It took a little convincing, she says, but Kitchener finally agreed to allow her to put the cuff on his arm. "He wasn't in the habit of bathing every day so he was likely feeling a little uncomfortable about that, not wanting to pull up his sleeves," she says. "So I put it over his sweater, and took his blood pressure. It was perfect. One twenty over seventy, just like he was eighteen years of age."

At the time Kitchener was already seventy-seven, but as Edie Bogle says, he certainly didn't have too many arterial or cholesterol problems.

She also asked him what he did when he was sick or had a toothache. He replied that he didn't get sick and when he had a toothache, he just kept working at the bothersome tooth until he could get it out. Edie recalls that he didn't have all his teeth and guesses that he had just pulled out those that were missing.

She wrote up her experiences, assembled photographs of Kitchener and put them together for an in-service presentation she offered to the staff at Harper University Hospital in Michigan, where she nursed for thirty years. The story of Kitchener elicited so much interest among her colleagues that Edie says she repeated it twice, and every year when she returned to the United States from her summer in Nova Scotia the first question she was asked was not about herself and her holiday but "What's the news from Kitchener?"

"He always told us, 'I have two doctors,'" reports Lloyd Bogle. "'I have my left leg and my right leg.' He always had answers just like that; you had to see the double meaning. He meant that he walked through the woods and that kept him healthy."

In 1995 or 1996 – Sergeant David Darrah of the Truro detachment of the RCMP is not sure which – a friend of Kitchener's called the police to say that he thought Willard might have died because it had been a long time since he had been seen in Earltown. It was February, says Sergeant Darrah, and the snow was very deep, so it would have been almost impossible to get to Gully Lake quickly overland. As a result, he says, he contacted the Nova Scotia Department of Natural Resources and negotiated the use of one of their helicopters from Shubenacadie, to go in to check on him.

The police officers and a Natural Resources worker flew in and found Kitchener suffering from flu-like symptoms in his hut. He resisted their offers to take him out for medical care, and then their efforts to get him out of his hut. It took three men to get him out and into the helicopter, according to Sergeat Darrah, who adds, "We had to pry him off the pole in the centre of his hovel."

They took him to the Colchester Regional Hospital in Truro, getting him in at about three p.m. for a full bath and medical examination and then back home, with a stop for groceries in Earltown, by eleven o'clock that night. "He even walked home on his own," adds Sergeant Darrah.

There is still a great deal of controversy about that forced medical evacuation and the lasting effects it may have had on Kitchener, who still seemed so in fear of any authorities. Sergeant Darrah dismisses any controversy, saying he had met Kitchener frequently over the years before that incident and the man had come to know he meant him no harm.

True to form, Kitchener didn't divulge a lot about this excursion and what he did tell friends could differ a great deal from one telling to another. He offered his friends conflicting versions of how he was transported, which hospital he was taken to and whether he found the experience traumatic or rather fun.

According to Lloyd Bogle, Kitchener complained about being forced into the helicopter. Lloyd feels that this was a traumatic experience for his old friend, and that it was this that led to his great fear later in life of being forced into a hospital or a senior citizens' home. For Lloyd, it also helped explain why, despite the fact that Kitchener often spoke about going on a little outing to Tatamagouche or River John, he usually wound up backing down. Lloyd recalls one exception, however. That was the day that Kitchener happily accompanied Lloyd and a television crew from ATV to Tatamagouche, and equally gladly allowed them to buy him some tobacco and a can of Pepsi – the drink to which his father Howard had always been partial.

Ruth Smith's understanding was that he greatly enjoyed the helicopter ride, and would later use it as a bargaining chip when friends wished to get him out to a hospital. In the last year of Kitchener's life he spent a cold night in the woods and when David Smith found him in the morning, he was concerned his old friend might be suffering from exposure. David called for an ambulance but when it arrived, Kitchener refused to get in, saying he would not go unless they sent the "airplane" again.

Of course he could be, as many friends say, very mischievous. So it's impossible to know whether he was demanding another evacuation by air as a ruse to avoid going anywhere near a hospital or doctor a second time, or whether he really did hope to get himself another ride in a helicopter.

He also seems to have had great difficulty saying outright "no" to those who wished to help him; it was as if he still respected all he'd learned as a child about good manners and gracious ways of dealing with well-meaning offers he didn't wish to accept.

Asked by his mother all those times to come out and live with her in Loch Broom, he never said no; he said he would "think about it." He gave the same kind of oblique answers to Lillie Stewart when she and her husband Jarvis invited him to come out with them and live in a very small, private cabin on their property in the woods near Stewiacke. Each time they visited him in the 1980s and 1990s they renewed their offer to take him out and set him up in the cabin. And each time they offered him this comfortable refuge, Lillie says he had the same reply. "'Well, that would be very nice,' he would say. Which meant no thank you, in other words," says Lillie. "But he never said that directly."

Lillie recalls his good manners, like those of a well-bred gentleman of a bygone era. He took pains to wait for her on the difficult path to and from his cabin, to escort her over the small, treacherous bridges of planks and logs across the brooks. And he didn't like to appear ungrateful for kindness offered.

So it may well be that his stated wish for another helicopter ride was just another polite way of saying "no" to another unsolicited medical evacuation.

Hector MacKenzie thinks his friend didn't think much of the chopper trip to the hospital, and with a laugh, recalls Kitchener, aghast, telling him that they had wanted to take off even his boots in that hospital.

"But I wouldn't let them do that," Kitchener said to Hector. "Because my socks was as old as my boots."

His lack of hygiene may also have helped him cope with the scourge of mosquitoes, black flies, deer flies and other insects that abound in northern Nova Scotia, especially in the swampy area around Gully Lake. He was constantly covered head to toe with soot and smoke from the woodstove in his hut. His hair and beard were matted and rarely washed, and even if there were times he was covered with mosquitoes, it seems he was either immune to their bites or perhaps the accumulated grime on his skin and hair deterred the insects from biting, acting as a natural insect repellent.

Like many toughened people used to a hard life in the woods, Kitchener didn't exactly subscribe to the relatively recent prescriptions for a long and healthy life. While he certainly never suffered any of the health problems associated with a modern sedentary life and too much food, he did smoke and drink right to the end.

Everyone remembers Kitchener's special fondness for tobacco, some special leaf tobacco that had to be ordered in from Montreal according to some versions, from Prince Edward Island according to others. On some occasions when Lloyd Bogle was visiting with friends and they offered Kitchener cigars, he gladly accepted those as well, although he was quite particular about what tobacco he did smoke, and would sometimes turn down offers of brands he didn't know or felt were inferior.

"He said he'd sooner be out of grub than out of tobacco," says Lloyd.

Hector MacKenzie laughs as he recounts his tale of Kitchener and cigars. He had gone back to Gully Lake to visit with two friends from Cape Breton, and when they got there, Kitchener said he wanted to go out to the store in Earltown. So they drove him down and Hector recalls that Kitchener picked up only a small bag of flour, the price of which was noted on a board on the wall. But Kitchener decided he wanted to "treat the boys who brought me out" and asked for four cigars from a display case in the window.

This was when Kitchener's aunt Etta Silver was covering the bill for the few foodstuffs Kitchener obtained at the Earltown General Store. But Hector says that did not include tobacco, so there were to be no cigars that day. The Cape Breton boys went without and so did Kitchener.

About a year later, Hector says, "The boys from Cape Breton were here again and we went out [to Gully Lake] again. And as soon as we got there, we went down to the store in Earltown. Now Social Services had taken Kitchener over and he could get anything he wanted. Well, he went through that store and he filled a bag and Murphy asked him if he wanted another one and he filled two bags. There were some cigars in the window there, and Kitchener reached out and took all the cigars there were. He was going to treat the boys this time. The government was paying this time. He had to make two trips back to the cabin, that time. He was living high on the hog!"

Kitchener comes out of the General Store in Earltown with his sack of supplies. (Photo by Lloyd Bogle)

In March 1982, during an afternoon of music and talk with Lloyd Bogle and David Buckler, Kitchener said that when he did buy cigars, he liked to smoke "White Owls" and promptly performed a remarkable owl call. Then he said, "What is that Mark Twain said? I'd sooner smoke in this world than in the next."

When he could get one, Kitchener also liked to take a drink when he was with friends and playing music, like many a Nova Scotian. In his younger years, he and Melvin MacKay had done some bootlegging of the moonshine they made, and it seems he continued to make his own drinks for years to come.

One eyewitness recalls a day he went in to see him along with Jessie and his brother Ronald, and Ronald went on ahead to bring Kitchener out to the car where his mother was waiting for him. Ronald had gone in stone cold sober, but when he and Kitchener appeared a little while later, they were both "pretty much out of it." Kitchener was talking all sorts of "crazy stuff" and his mother kept asking him what was wrong with him.

Alone in the woods as he was for so much of the time, he obviously had very little access to store-bought alcohol, so he always seemed happy to accept a drink brought to him by friends. His cautious approach to food gifts didn't seem to apply to liquor.

Lloyd Bogle and Hector MacKenzie always arrived with a bottle or two, Lloyd bringing beer or wine and Hector taking along a little rum. On Lloyd's audiotapes, in between the fiddling and singing, Kitchener can be heard musing about how little alcohol there was in commercially brewed beer. One afternoon when Lloyd was there with a fellow musician, he convinced Kitchener to divulge his own secret recipe for what he called his "shine."

"You get water on the stove to boiling, with barley in the jug, then you put molasses on top of that," said Kitchener. "That's warm water and you let it sit there for about two weeks. It's just about forty percent. One cup full, two cups full you start talking to yourself," he added, with a laugh.

He was not, by any accounts, a natural talker and it seems the liquor and music together would loosen him up, allow him to let down his guard and overcome his suspicion and fear of the outside world.

Dave Buckler had the strong impression that Kitchener really trusted no one, that he was torn between his love of music, company and fun, and his need for solitude. "Definitely, he craved people but there was something keeping him away from associating with other people," he says. "He yearned for privacy, wanting to be alone, and he enjoyed nature and the remoteness from other people."

Edie Bogle described him as a timid man, with fears that bordered on paranoia. These may well have been the natural result of his many years of isolation as well as engrained anxieties that others were out to take advantage of him.

Certainly, if he did trust anyone, they were very few – in keeping with the adage he passed on to Ruth Smith's children in Loganville, about speaking little and trusting but few. The Smith family, Lloyd MacIntosh and Murphy Stonehouse were among the select group he seemed to trust the most, possibly because he had known them for so much of his life.

Occasionally he would make his way down the paths on the north side of Gully Lake to visit the Smiths, and to go, as David Smith puts it, on a "toot." He recalls the one that Kitchener went on a few months before his cabin burned down in 2003. In keeping with his refusal to spend the night away from his own Gully Lake home, Kitchener had headed home late one very cold afternoon, after one of these heavy drinking sessions. The Smiths worried about him all night because of the cold weather and because of his advanced age – he was, after all, eighty-six years old. In the morning David found him asleep by a tree on the path. He had torn off most of his clothing, which was scattered "helter-skelter" around him. But he had obviously been extremely cold and confused; when David came across him he had a glove on one foot.

David dressed him up in a cap and sweater his mother had given him, which may well have saved his life. David then put Kitchener on his ATV and took him as far as the four-wheeler could go up that rocky path. He was very concerned that Kitchener was suffering from hypothermia after that night in the open, and tried to convince his friend to allow him to piggy-back him the remaining three hundred metres to his hut. But Kitchener, stubborn and proud as ever, refused to be carried and insisted on making his own way home. David went on ahead to light the fire in the stove and to get the hut warmed up for Kitchener's arrival. And then he went back and checked on his friend, who still refused any help. Kitchener crawled home on his hands and knees. It took him three hours.

Concerned that his old friend might catch pneumonia, David then went to Earltown to call for a doctor and an ambulance was dispatched to pick up Kitchener. And this is when Kitchener refused to get into the ambulance, saying he would only go if they sent out a helicopter to fetch him, as they had years earlier for the unsolicited medical check-up ordered up by Social Services and worried friends.

He was, as they say, his own man, determined to be master of his own destiny.

Kitchener (left) with his friend Lloyd Bogle. (Photo courtesy Lloyd Bogle)

Chapter 11
Many helping hands and many visitors

Kitchener certainly had remarkable survival skills and strength to have endured the hardship of his life at Gully Lake, but a great deal of credit also goes to the many people in the community and indeed all over the province who provided him with a safety net. This included unquestioning friendship and also quietly supplying him with things he needed over the years without eroding his pride or dignity – tools, food, musical instruments such as fiddle and guitars, books and magazines, batteries and flashlights, bottles and tobacco, snowshoes, skis, bicycles, reading glasses. It is a tribute to the people of northern Nova Scotia that they rallied around him – from a distance that safeguarded his privacy – to ensure that he did not suffer more than he absolutely had to, given his choice of a reclusive life in the hills.

Before Social Services took over, Kitchener's aunt Etta Silver, whose husband was the inspector of schools in Nova Scotia, covered the costs of the few staples he picked up from time to time in the Earltown store. But she was just one of many who helped him out over the years. Ruth Smith would offer him her homemade biscuits and sent staples back with him when he left. His many friends – both from his youth and ones who sought him out in the last three decades of his life – never came empty-handed, asking him what he needed and ensuring that he didn't run out of essentials. Frequently they took him out to Earltown for groceries to save him the long trip on foot or skis or bicycle. Many helped him cut and stack firewood that allowed him to make it through the hard and long winters up in the woods.

While Murphy Stonehouse in Earltown doesn't like to talk about it himself, preferring as he says, "to stay in the background," everyone in the community agrees that he was extremely generous over the years to Willard Kitchener MacDonald. He is probably one of a very few who really knew the man rather than the legend, accepted him exactly as he was and went to great lengths to ensure he did not suffer.

Giving to Kitchener was not always easy, according to Ruth Smith and Hector MacKenzie. Ruth says she had to insist that he not pay her for things she gave him, and as Hector says, he didn't always accept the offerings of food he took up to him. In his early visits, Hector says he and his friends would take him sweets but he wouldn't accept them, saying he didn't care for too much sugar. Then, in later years when they went in to Earltown, Kitchener himself would always make sure he got a bag of chocolate chip cookies that he would eat on the way home to Gully Lake.

In the 1970s, when Lloyd Bogle and his group of friends from all over Colchester and Cumberland Counties befriended Kitchener, he often told them that he needed money. Perhaps by this time, he was less able to provide for himself and bring in a little income the way he had in the 1950s by peddling soap and moonshine or his axe handles and pelts from his traplines. Whatever the reason, in those recorded conversations in 1982, a recurring theme is his need for money. Then Lloyd Bogle or Dave Buckler would attempt to convince him that he could receive money through social welfare if only he would agree to come out with them and make an application to the government.

His stated need for money led many to believe that all that was still keeping him in the woods was his own lack of it, and in 1982, he said to Lloyd, "If I had enough money I'd go out. I wouldn't want to put you through the life I've had."

"No doubt about it, everyone likes to have money," said Kitchener. "Only some people make a god out of it. When it does that, you're in danger."

To Dave Buckler, Kitchener once said he hated living where he lived, and to Dave's wife, Corrine Trites, he said, "I'd give anything to move to the village [Earltown]." But both Dave and his wife believe he may have been telling them what he thought they wanted to hear. On one level, they believe he may indeed have thought sometimes it would be nice to have an easier life on the "outside," but he also knew he would not fit back into a life where he would be expected to mingle with people all the time, not after all those years on his own.

Many times in the 1970s and '80s he expressed his need for money. It's not clear whether he meant the money he felt he was owed by those mysterious people who had stolen his ideas, songs and stories, as remuneration he felt he deserved, or just for the things he wanted but could not have without some source of income, such as tobacco and perhaps musical instruments.

So Lloyd Bogle, Dave Buckler and several other friends in the area and in Truro, including Jarvis and Lillie Stewart, began to investigate the ins and outs of getting some social assistance for Kitchener. At first, they met with enormous resistance or indifference from Kitchener himself. They would explain to him how the government worked, how social welfare benefits worked, and Kitchener would repeatedly ask whether this would be an acknowledgement of the money he had not been paid for his inventions and ideas.

Understandably, Kitchener had very little comprehension of the way governments now worked in Canada – although many of us can probably say the same thing. He also seemed to have very little faith that any government or authorities would actually be willing to provide him with any money at all.

His friends would explain that the government took money from the people in the form of taxes, which was then used to provide assistance to those who needed it, to make life a little easier for them.

After a long explanation to that effect one day in 1982, his friends asked Kitchener if he understood that.

"Oh, I think so," he replied. Then, "Is it true that we are governed by Nazis?"

"No, no," replied Lloyd Bogle. "We're governed by ourselves, Dave, aren't we? Bobby, Dave, me, Kitchener. We are the government, because we elect it."

Kitchener was quiet for a moment. Then he said, "Ever hear this saying? Crime will not decrease until it becomes more dangerous to be a criminal than a victim? I read that in a book."

Kitchener's reference points were very different from those of people living within the system, watching it develop around them and obliged to file income tax returns, keep paper trails, manage personal finances with banks and credit cards and all the many trappings of our modern world. His world involved the nature around him and the odd assortment of facts, figures and ideas he found in books, magazines and newspapers. There was little to connect him to the work-a-day world on the outside. He wanted a little money, probably to make him feel independent, but that didn't mean he wanted to be drawn into any complex relationship with the very authorities he had distrusted for half a century.

But by then, the ball was set in motion and many people went to great lengths to secure government assistance for Kitchener. Not all of those who helped out are even on record.

Ed Lorraine, MLA for the constituency of Colchester County from 1981 until 1999 and one-time Minister of Agriculture for the province, was eventually solicited to try to help get some social assistance for Kitchener. He recalls going back to visit him in his camp at Gully Lake to try to convince him to sign for government money. Kitchener refused to sign anything, ever. Eventually Ed went out to Earltown and talked to Murphy Stonehouse, to tell him to give Kitchener what he wanted and to send the bill to Social Services in Truro.

"What groceries he got never amounted to a hill of beans," says Ed Lorraine. "I doubt his bill was even twenty dollars a month." He says that Kitchener had an American birth certificate, but that he had come to Canada very young and had lived in the country his whole life and thus he deserved the social security benefits he was given.

He gives the credit for this and for the later wrangling with Ottawa to secure Kitchener's old age pension for which he qualified in 1981, to the then Director of Social Services in Truro, Betty Thompson. As unbelievable as it may now seem, she was able to convince Ottawa to dispense an old age pension for Willard Kitchener MacDonald, without his ever signing a single piece of paper.

But the problems didn't end there. Once the pension had been secured, cheques were sent out to Kitchener and he refused to sign them so they went uncashed. Once again, Social Services in Truro found a solution by having the pension put into a trust fund set up for Kitchener by the Municipality of Colchester County, and using that to refund any purchases he made at the General Store in Earltown.

Jarvis and Lillie Stewart, whom Lloyd Bogle had introduced to Kitchener in the 1980s, were present in 1986 when Lloyd along with a CBC crew went in, hoping to get Kitchener to sign for his pension while the television cameras captured the event – in vain, as it turned out. Lillie now thinks the approach was "all wrong," and that if it had been done differently, if someone had explained to Kitchener that each month he would have received a certain amount of money, he might have signed. She had a feeling that the County was anxious he get that pension from Ottawa because this would remove their obligation to use Social Services money, coming then from the County budget, to cover his grocery bills, as small as they were.

"I mean, he didn't have to have six hundred dollars a month to supply him with that," says Lillie. "So I was ticked with the people who went in there again and again, and every time I would hear about another group going in, [I would] imagine what he's going through with these people . . . trying to get him to sign. Why didn't they leave him alone, is all I could say." She thinks he didn't really need the money, or else he would have signed for it.

Still, the pension was secured, the trust fund set up and managed by the County. It would be money from this fund that would eventually be used to construct a small cabin for Kitchener near the Kemptown Road.

After many years of great solitude during which Kitchener really did live the life of a hermit, in the 1980s and 1990s his life began to change dramatically. By now, he had begun to tweak many imaginations; people were fascinated by this elusive and mysterious man living in isolation in the woods, and his legend was growing. Many wanted to know how he had survived up in that wilderness camp, which now – juxtaposed against the "total electric lives" of people in the modern and economically flourishing Canada – defied most imaginations. The more people began to seek him out, the more his privacy was eroded as his life became the subject of speculation, rumour and many conflicting tales, some of them far taller than the man himself. Ironically, he helped these stories grow with the idiosyncratic comments he made to journalists about the world, nature, his own inventions, science, the Bible, and life itself. Over time, he seems to have become more used to strangers dropping in to see him, and to have come up with a whole range of intriguing ideas, stories and jokes he trotted out to entertain his guests.

Ruth Smith figures that while he probably rather liked the attention, she wasn't so sure he liked the name "Hermit of Gully Lake." She thought some of the journalists involved were "pretty rude." Along with the attention, came some unwelcome myths and unflattering stories that seriously offended the Smiths and others close to Kitchener.

"One of my grandchildren said even his teacher said in school that he [the Hermit] lives alone with the animals and that he couldn't talk," says Ruth. "He [Ruth's grandson] said, 'I was just furious but I didn't dare to open my mouth 'cause if I did I'd be put out of school.'"

In the way of journalists (and people who write books) everywhere, they (and I) certainly pried into his private life in a way that his long-time friends would never have dreamed of doing. They – like I – sought answers to questions that friends didn't dare or wish to ask: how he bathed; what had made him stay in the woods; whether he worried about growing old. Mostly, he answered their questions, often surprisingly candidly, often in an enigmatic way that added to the mystery and the myths that were growing around him.

By the 1980s, Gully Lake had also become a favourite recreation area for ATV and snowmobile clubs, and just as Kitchener didn't always appear to welcome visitors, he didn't always welcome this new traffic and intrusion on his privacy either. Such intrusions seemed to heighten his sense of mischief, already being fanned by the attention he was getting.

He told friends how one winter's night when the snow was deep, a group of young men on snowmobiles actually ran right into his little cabin. The way Kitchener recounted the story, the young rowdies woke him up and annoyed him. So he quietly opened his door/window and thrust his head and arms through the small opening, crying in a strangled voice, "It's a good night for MURDER!"

That was the last he saw of that group of young men and their snowmobiles. They high-tailed it off into the night, bashing into trees in their panic to flee.

David Smith says that Kitchener had driven motorcycles and cars in his youth, before moving back to Gully Lake, and that he once got on a friend's snowmobile and drove it pell-mell down the road, making his friends fear he would crash. According to David, Kitchener even went in to Tatamagouche once to look at buying a snowmobile himself, but the proprietor of the dealership there managed to dissuade him, worried that he would hurt himself.

Lloyd Bogle recalls that one day Kitchener announced to him that he would like to go to Tatamagouche to buy an all terrain vehicle. He then pulled from his pocket a World Money Order worth nine hundred dollars given to him by his relatives, Etta and B.C. Silver, and which Lloyd says he carried on him most of the time. Lloyd told him it wasn't enough, and that he would have to get some money from his trust fund if he wanted to buy an ATV. But when Lloyd asked Kitchener about it next time he went back, Kitchener claimed he had lost the money order. On a subsequent visit, Kitchener said he had found the World Money Order again, but there was no more talk about buying an ATV, probably because it would have meant dealing with the authorities to get hold of the additional money he would need from that trust fund.

And so, unless friends were there to drive him out in their cars or on their own snowmobiles or ATVs, Kitchener continued to make his way into Earltown and down to Loganville or even over to River John on one of his two bicycles, when weather permitted it, on skis and snowshoes when the snow was deep. One of these bicycles, which is still leaning on a tree in the woods near Gully Lake, Kitchener considered jinxed, according to David Smith, because every time he went to get on it, it seemed to have a flat tire. At some point, he had adorned the handlebars of that supposedly accursed bicycle with a small Canadian flag that was still there in October 2004, long after he himself was not – at least not in body.

Although he kept it in check when women were present, he had an occasionally naughty – even raunchy – sense of humour that he would share during those long afternoons of music and conversation with the men who went up to spend time with him.

A few of these jokes and stories, some too politically incorrect and risqué to repeat here, have been captured on Lloyd's audio cassettes, and Kitchener prefaces them with a cautionary note not to repeat them to the "ladies in church."

One joke that can be repeated here Kitchener told this way: "There was a school teacher and in the school yard there was an old stack of boards that he thought were dangerous for the kids to play around. So the teacher told a young boy to put up a sign to warn the kids not to go near those old boards. And it didn't do any good so the teacher went out to see what the sign said. And the boy had written, 'It is dangerous to play around old broads.'"

While there were occasions when Kitchener would make audacious claims about his many inventions and the lack of recognition for these, more often than not he leaned towards self-deprecation. He would claim, even after he had told a good joke, that he was a little slow to pick up these stories and to understand them. But he still had quite a repertoire of stories to tell.

"A fella gave his wife a million dollars to go out and spend a thousand dollars a day, and three years later she come back and wanted some more. This time he gave her a billion dollars. And she didn't come back for three hundred years."

Asked his age, he might quote Jack Benny: "Jack Benny, whenever anyone asked his age, he always said twenty-nine," Kitchener quipped one day. "Well, years passed and he always said the same thing. There was another old lady, when people asked her how old she was, she would always say plenty-nine."

Hector MacKenzie laughs himself hoarse over some of the yarns that Kitchener spun. He had made up several different versions of an encounter with a bear, and Hector confirms there were indeed real encounters with bears – he himself had seen the tracks and the spot where the bear had urinated right in front of the Gully Lake cabin. But, storyteller that he was, Kitchener liked to embellish the truth. He described the bear sticking its snout right through the window into his cabin, where Kitchener claims he hit it on the nose because he didn't want to shoot it. And Kitchener's cousin Shirley recalls the version that he told her, about how, after he hit the bear on the nose he told a funny joke that made the bear laugh so hard it fell down and died.

"He didn't expect us to take his jokes serious," says Hector.

Chapter 12
The spiritual dimension

When Jessie's niece, Shirley Sutherland Miller, went in to see Kitchener in 2000, she had not seen or spoken to her cousin since her early childhood when her parents used to take her to visit the MacDonald family in Pictou.

Shirley was very moved by the reunion, and judging from the series of photographs that Lloyd snapped that day of Kitchener as he guardedly studied, recognized, then threw an arm around and embraced his long-lost cousin – so was he. Those photographs with his cousin are some of the very rare ones in which Kitchener is smiling openly.

"There was something in his eyes," says Shirley, struggling to find words for the powerful impact Kitchener had on her. She was struck by the way he would cup his hand on his chin and contemplate in silence before speaking or replying to a question, a gesture uncannily like one her own father, Kitchener's maternal uncle, used.

Shirley was particularly impressed by Kitchener's way with words, the many sayings and words of wisdom that were always at the tip of his tongue. She was also the one who took note of – and found a meaning in – the five snowmen that Kitchener made just in

Kitchener smiles with his cousin Shirley Sutherland Miller, whom he had not seen since the 1940s. (Photo by Lloyd Bogle)

front of his cabin every winter, adorning these neat pillars of snow with stones for eyes.

She believes that the snowmen represented Kitchener and his family – his father who had died in 1971, his mother who had died in 1980, his "brother" Ronald who died in 2001 and his sister Kathleen who died when he was still a young man. Despite his decision to live alone in the woods, Shirley believes he had deep feelings for his family. She compiled a magnificent scrapbook featuring Kitchener and his family, and in recent years researched their common Sutherland ancestry on her father's side and his mother's, with genealogical research that stretched back to Scotland.

She says her Uncle Howard was a musical genius and craftsman, talents he passed on to his son. She also believes that Kitchener's deep faith and his intense reading of the Bible were things he had learned in his home from his parents. After the tragic fire that

Five snowmen: friends say he often made five snow figures like these in the winters. Kitchener's cousin Shirley Sutherland Miller believes they represented his family – father Howard, mother Jessie, sister Kathleen, "brother" Ronald, and himself. (Photo by Lloyd Bogle)

burned his hut in 2003, she gave him her late parents' family Bible. Hector MacKenzie says before that, he too had noticed that Kitchener's Bible was in pretty rough shape so he took one from church to replace it.

Kitchener's religious faith remains, not surprisingly, something of a puzzle – just like the man himself. His Bible was always very important to him; he seemed to read it intensely, try to comprehend the messages there and to obey them. He quoted the sixth commandment that forbids killing in reply to any questions about his jump from the troop train. And he said that the Bible prescribed the snow baths he took.

Ruth Smith describes him as a "religious" man, like his mother who was close to her Bible. But she says he didn't attend any church.

Others report that he went out to River John on occasion, or at least he said he wanted to, to thank church women there who had been so good to his mother over the years. Robert Clark says Kitchener asked him the last time he saw him, in 2003, if he could help him get some money to "some religion." But he didn't specify which one and the matter went no further.

In October 1991, during an afternoon of music with Bobby Matheson and Lloyd Bogle, Kitchener said that he tried hard to understand science and the world, but they remained a mystery to him and the Bible seemed to be full of contradictions and "a lot of strange names."

"Do you believe there's a God?" asked Lloyd.

"Oh definitely," Kitchener replied. "I didn't used to, but I do now."

The morning rituals that he told friends he performed each day, which included chanting, certainly suggest that he had strong spiritual beliefs. Pastor Neil Stirling, who delivered the eulogy at his funeral in Earltown, says he believes Kitchener had become a born-again Christian before he died. He never met Kitchener, but he did spend a lot of time learning about him from those who knew him well in Earltown and who in recent years had become born-again Christians.

Pastor Stirling offers a story told to him in an e-mail from Scott Campbell, a Christian living in Truro, about Kitchener and a Bible. A teen group from Crossroads Baptist Church in Truro had visited Kitchener, taking him some food and a Bible written in simple English because they were not sure of his reading level. Kitchener gladly received the food but said that he already owned a Bible, so perhaps it could be given to someone without one.

"I was leaving the next week for Brazil on a short-term missions trip," wrote Scott Campbell to Pastor Stirling, "so the teen group gave me the Bible and asked if I could find someone there to give it to. So . . . I took it with me. Once in Brazil, I realized that everyone spoke Portuguese! I had an English Bible to give away."

Scott's tale continues: "Late in our trip, a young man named Saul (how fitting!) did some translation work for us. He was not a Christian but his English was excellent. I became convinced that Saul was the perfect recipient for the Bible – so I told him the story of the teen group and that I had this English Bible to give away – and that

I would like him to have it. He gratefully received it, saying he had never owned a Bible before. The next day, he came to the work site, and said he had gone home and read the entire Gospel of John, and was convinced that Jesus was who He claimed to be, and [Saul now] . . . trusted Christ for his salvation."

"So in his own way, through his generosity," wrote Scott Campbell, "Willard was able to 'evangelize' someone in Brazil – and God, through His providence, placed a Bible version in simple English in the hands of a young man who knew only simple English."

Neil Stirling thinks that Willard Kitchener MacDonald was important spiritually for many people who knew him and cared about him – people in the community and even further away with whom he had a symbiotic relationship. And he describes Kitchener and his friend Murphy Stonehouse as "two geniuses out in the bush."

Whatever the actual nature of his own spiritual leanings, Kitchener did have a remarkable effect on many of those who went to visit him. Some found in him an ability to soothe their spiritual troubles or even to inspire belief in his own deep spiritual powers. This is not an uncommon phenomenon with hermits and recluses the world over, who seem to offer the promise of great wisdom and peace of mind to people caught up in and deeply troubled by the stresses and tensions of daily life on the "outside."

Just as many people rallied around Kitchener and gave freely to him, he seems to have fulfilled a need in many of the lives he touched.

Chapter 13
A new hermitage

In the 1990s, having secured a pension for Kitchener, many of his friends and those in Social Services who kept an eye on his welfare, began to worry about his advancing age and the years to come when he would no longer be able to get in and out of the tiny window/door in his hut, or even make it out to Earltown or down to Loganville from his hermitage at Gully Lake. More and more, they worried about his ability to survive the harsh winters in the woods. Kitchener himself had said that although he was still able to snare rabbits to supply a little meat, there were far fewer deer in the area and fish in the lake than there once had been, and the moose were long gone.

When Lillie Stewart asked him how he was going to cope when he got too old to climb in and out of his cabin, or offered him hats and boots for when it got too cold, he would turn to her with a slightly puzzled look and say, "You worry an awful lot."

Some of his friends continued to try to convince him to move out of the woods and into Earltown, while others thought he should consider giving himself a long-overdue break and a life with comforts by moving into a seniors' home. Perhaps because Kitchener himself continued to quietly oppose any such idea, his well-wishers then came up with a whole new idea – build him a new cabin with at least a few amenities where he could live out his remaining years in comfort they thought he might appreciate after half a century of very rough living.

It was another example of the extent to which people in the community had come to care for their old reclusive friend, and how municipal and provincial government officials were willing to bend rules and make exceptions to accommodate him. It also shows the level of solidarity that still exists in many rural areas. While in some parts of the world, hermits are shunned or feared, especially by governments, in northern Nova Scotia it seemed many people were very intent on protecting and helping out their own increasingly famous hermit.

In October 1996 Rosalind Penfound, Director of Land Administration in Nova Scotia's Department of Natural Resources, wrote an official letter to the northern regional office of the Department of the Environment, "requesting permission to utilize an area of Crown land on Gully Lake Road, Colchester County, to construct a temporary residence for Mr. Willard Kitchener MacDonald."

There were several caveats attached, among them the stipulation that the structure be constructed and maintained solely by Mr. MacDonald as a temporary residence and for no other purpose.

"The only structures permitted on site shall be the residence and an outside privy which shall meet all acceptable building codes," said the letter. "This authority shall be for the lifetime of Mr. Willard Kitchener MacDonald and shall continue automatically from year to year unless earlier terminated by the Minister of Natural Resources. This authority cannot be transferred. The authority shall immediately terminate upon the demise or relocation of Mr. Willard Kitchener MacDonald and the land shall revert to the Department of Natural Resources. All structures shall, at that time, be removed within sixty days of the demise or relocation of Mr. MacDonald. Should, upon the demise of Mr. MacDonald, any heirs claim an interest in the structures, they shall be advised of the conditions of removal."

There were a host of other conditions, including an interdiction on the cutting of any trees other than those that had to be removed in constructing the cabin, and one stipulating that the site be maintained in a "clean and wholesome condition."

With his irregular and modest purchases in Earltown, Kitchener was hardly making a dent in his pension, which was being channelled directly into the trust fund being administered for him by the municipality, so there was no shortage of money to build the cabin and to put in a well next to it.

The new structure would turn out to be a one-and-a-half storey cabin, replete with a loft that served as a bedroom, basic furniture, and a small kitchen area with a sink. The idea for the loft, according to Shirley Sutherland Miller, came from Kitchener himself, in consultation with "Clem" (not his real name), a man who had known Kitchener well and who had been close to his brother Ronald since childhood. Perhaps the loft reminded Kitchener of the attic in the Pictou house where he once lived at least some of the time with his family.

According to Shirley, Kitchener also wanted a desk in his new cabin because he said he was going to write a book.

Then the cabin was completed, right down to a brand new mattress on a real bed in the loft. An airtight woodstove on the main floor would reduce his need for firewood and the charcoal he made himself from green wood, and the dirty work of stoking a makeshift stove that left his hands and his face permanently covered with black soot. A sort of house-warming party was organized with several friends and government people who had gone out of their way to see the project through from start to finish. Even a large cake was baked.

The only thing missing was Kitchener himself.

After all those comments over the years about wanting to move "out," Kitchener didn't like the new cabin. He spent one or two nights there in 2002, then headed back to his own hut in the woods, saying the red cottage was too noisy and too close to the road. Lloyd Bogle figured he went along with the project only to keep people from "bugging him too much."

The Red Cabin, built using Kitchener's old age pension from a trust fund set up by the Municipality of Colchester County. Kitchener lived here in the final months of his life. The bag hanging on the doorknob contains beans and garlic brought by friends worried about his health; he disappeared without removing the bag.
(Photo by Joan Baxter)

In his absence, the place was robbed; the woodstove and furniture were stolen and the County began to appoint caretakers to keep an eye on it. Lloyd spent one night on duty there with his shotgun, hoping in vain the culprits who had stolen from Kitchener's new cabin would return.

They didn't, and neither did Kitchener. At least not just yet.

Leroy Marshall figures the place just wasn't right for his father, who had never asked for a well, didn't need one and who had always drunk water right from Gully Lake. Kitchener would ignore the well and continue to drink from the brook that ran behind the cabin even after he moved into it later.

"And the toilet," adds Ruth Smith. "He didn't need no toilet. They were thinking more in their terms than in Willard's."

Shirley recalls her cousin telling her that he had tried to sleep in the bed up in the loft, but that he found it too slippery and fell off it during the night. When she went up to check, she found that he had left the plastic on the new mattress, and she told him he would need to take that off. But in the end he preferred just to set that mattress aside. He had not slept on a mattress for so many years, he obviously saw no reason for one now.

So after just a night or two in his new "home," Kitchener headed back up the hill to his own familiar hermitage in the woods a stone's throw from Gully Lake. There he felt comfortable, even if his idea of what comfort meant was certainly not shared by many other people. And there he remained, surrounded by his small collection of personal treasures and the woodlands he knew so well, until Wednesday, May 21, 2003.

On that day, tragedy struck. The makeshift chimney he had rigged up on his stove caught fire and his hut burned to the ground, as did about forty hectares of woodland on the north side of Gully Lake. Fortunately, Kitchener was not trapped inside. Unfortunately, he was not able to save anything from the conflagration that sent nearly all his books, his own jotted notes on paper, his old guitar and the new fiddle he had recently been given, all that he owned and the life he knew, up in smoke.

Journalist Harry Sullivan arrived when the forest fire was still raging, to find Kitchener wandering about in front of his smouldering hut. Harry had grown up in Nuttby, and as far back as he could remember and even before he was born, he says, "Willard was a larger-than-life living legend around those small, surrounding, rural communities." In a lovely profile he wrote of him for the *Truro Daily News* in December 2003, Harry said, "Willard was someone you knew of but didn't know."

Willard Kitchener MacDonald on May 21, 2003, collecting remnants of clothing around the burned-out area where his hut has just burned to the ground.
(Photo by Harry Sullivan, courtesy of the *Truro Daily News*)

Despite attempts as a child to catch a glimpse of the old hermit and one unsuccessful foray into the woods at Gully Lake a few years earlier to try to have a journalistic chat with Kitchener, it wasn't until the day of the fire that Harry first laid eyes on the elusive old man.

"I'd have to say his mood was strange," says Harry. "He didn't seem overly excited at all. He was just standing there taking things in. A few bits of clothing – he gathered those up and started walking away. When I went up to talk to him, I was asking him about his being there and what he was going to do now. And his response was that he'd heard about all the wars that were raging in the outside world and he wanted to know if that was really true."

Harry still isn't sure which war or wars Kitchener was referring to – the American-led invasion of Iraq that U.S. president George W. Bush had just declared officially over or other conflicts linked to the American "War on Terror." Or perhaps he just viewed these as extensions of World War II, which, in some ways, they probably were.

"To Willard, the outside world was a place filled with war, deafening noises and confusion," wrote Harry Sullivan in his profile of Kitchener. "It filled him with fear and he wanted no part of it."

As far as Harry could see on the day of the fire, the only thing Kitchener was able to salvage from the ruins of his hovel were the bits of clothing he was picking up outside.

Shirley Sutherland Miller believes that someone may have managed to save his Bible, which was usually on the step outside. But she says everything else was lost and he was never the same after his hut burned to the ground. "He lost all his treasures, and they were treasures like you wouldn't believe," she says. "He wrote things down, and he did say he was going to write a book one day with those. He was very sad about that; he spoke about it a lot."

"I remember he said he was writing a song about the seagull and the raven," she says. "And he asked us what we thought. He said maybe we would get it taped in case people might enjoy hearing it, not to make money. And we never got to see whether he wrote anything down. The raven and the seagull; we don't know how far it went in his head. We'll never know."

"One time I was sitting there, and he pointed out to the tree and there was a big raven out there and the sun was shining on the raven. And he started the story by saying, 'I think I'll dye my hair blue, what do you think?' And he did that little thing with his chin in his hand and then the sun came on the raven. There was a blue shade, 'fabulous' I think is the word he used, and he said, 'I think I'll dye my hair blue.' It was just precious. I should have written it down. His senses were in touch with nature that way."

Now, with his hut in ashes, Kitchener had little choice but to move down the hill to the red cabin the County had built for him using his pension fund. That is where he spent the summer and autumn of 2003.

Lloyd Bogle remembers a trip that summer. "We went in and he was laying out in the yard with his feet up in the air and his head on a big rock and he was reading a book, and the fella with me said, 'Why would you lay like that, Kitchener?' And Kitchener said, 'No particular reason.' His mind didn't work the way others' do."

The last time Lloyd saw him was in September 2003, when he took him a new guitar. Kitchener had complained that he was having trouble with a couple of guitars that people had given him after the fire. "I was with "Clem" and his son and his son's girlfriend, and there was maybe eleven people at one time on this Sunday afternoon," says Lloyd. "There was some neighbours and a couple from Truro, and we got him going on the new guitar and he was enjoying himself. He hadn't played a lot since the fire. That took a lot out of him, the fire."

As they had in the past, people in the community and even from elsewhere in the province rallied around the recluse in his time of need, when he moved into the cabin. Shirley brought some things from her own late parents' house in Truro – a kitchen clock, a birdhouse and her father's (Kitchener's uncle's) tools.

Willard Kitchener MacDonald
(Photo by Dr. Gerry Farrell)

"We asked him permission to put up the clock," she says. "And he thought about it and said, 'If you want to,' and I went over and held it up over the stove, and that was fine."

Next time she went back, however, she noticed that the clock was upside-down. "And I just got up and said, 'Oh look at your clock, Kitchener,' and I put it upright."

Next time she visited him, the clock was again upside-down. This time, rather than change it, she merely said to her cousin that his clock seemed to be upside-down. He performed his characteristic thinking pose with his hand cupping his chin and replied, "That's right, but the world is upside down anyway, don't you think?"

Chapter 14
Lost... then found

> Keep right on to the end of the road,
> Keep right on to the end,
> Tho' the way be long, let your heart be strong,
> Keep right on round the bend.
> Tho' you're tired and weary still journey on,
> Till you come to your happy abode,
> Where all the love you've been dreaming of
> Will be there at the end of the road.
>
> "Keep Right on to the End of the Road"
> written and composed by
> William Dillon and Sir Harry Lauder

The fall of 2003 was a turbulent one in Nova Scotia. It began with Hurricane Juan that cut a swath through the province in the early hours of September 29, unleashing its fury first on a stretch of coast from Musquodoboit Harbour in the east to Prospect in the west, and then blasting right across the mainland through Truro, over the hills to Gully Lake and then across Northumberland Strait to lash at Charlottetown on Prince Edward Island.

It is probably fortunate that Kitchener was already in his new cabin, and spared the devastation that the howling swirling winds of Hurricane Juan wrought around the lake, toppling trees that rendered the whole area and many of his old paths almost impassable.

November brought early snowstorms with heavy, wet snowfalls in the northeast of the province. And it also meant the onset of the annual flu season. And this time, Kitchener would not be spared. At least that is what many believe.

It's almost impossible to piece together the events leading up to his disappearance, even to know who was the last person to see him alive and who might have said what to make him flee his cabin and head off, ill as he was, up the long road to Gully Lake and then into the woods.

Great controversy surrounds his disappearance, how it was handled and what or who may have caused it in the first place. Most agree that he was ailing, suffering from a nasty flu as he told several friends who saw him in the days prior to his disappearance. But why did he leave his cabin when he was sick and go traipsing up the road towards Gully Lake? That is where opinions among his friends are sharply divided and in a few cases, so are the friends themselves who have no use for – or anything good to say about – each other.

Some think he decided completely on his own, without any pressure or fear of being taken in for medical treatment, to head up the Gully Lake Road, go literally and metaphorically to the "end of the road," to die surrounded by familiar landmarks and the nature that had been his constant companion for decades.

There are others who believe he was driven from his cabin by fear that one of his well-meaning friends might force him out to a hospital, or worse, into a seniors' home for the winter and perhaps for the rest of his days.

No one wishes to say who called out the police and the helicopters and the rescue teams that went in searching for him on Wednesday, December 3, 2003.

Shirley Sutherland Miller says that the last time she saw him was on the Sunday, November 30. She says "Clem," a long-time friend of the MacDonald family, had been in on the Saturday and that he had spoken to Kitchener about the medicinal properties of garlic in treating his illness. According to Shirley's account, Kitchener had asked "Clem" for some tobacco. So he had gone to Earltown to get tobacco but could not find the garlic, and he had driven all the way to Truro to find some garlic cloves, which he then took back to Kitchener, along with some beans and the tobacco. Kitchener didn't come to the door, so "Clem" had hung the plastic bag on the door handle and left. The man I'm calling Clem declined to be part of this book or to speak to me about Kitchener, so it is not possible to verify the exact events of that afternoon.

At some point, an ambulance with paramedics was called in. But Kitchener wouldn't let them even approach his cabin, reportedly threatening to shoot them if they came any closer.

On Sunday, to see how he was faring, Shirley went in to see Kitchener, accompanied by "Clem" and Dr. Gerry Farrell, who had always visited Kitchener as a friend, taken marvellous photographs of him, and never approached him in a medical capacity. They assured Kitchener they had no intention of forcing him to do anything he didn't want to, that they had just come to see how he was. Shirley says Kitchener spoke to them through the window, saying that he had the flu and he didn't want them to catch it from him. He did not open the door to let them in. The tobacco was gone from the bag, but the bag itself was still hanging from the doorknob; the cans of beans and garlic had not been removed.

"I don't know who saw him after that," says Shirley. "We saw him about three o'clock on Sunday, and I stood at the back window where the little stove was and everybody else went down the driveway, and I knocked, hoping he would let me come in. But he just ignored it and he went over to the stove and got a piece of wood and opened the little door, pushed the wood in. It wouldn't go all the way, and it was like he had a bit of temper, and he just opened the door and booted it in, and then this all happened in a few seconds, and I knocked again and he wouldn't move. So I turned around and went up the driveway too. That's the last I saw of him. So he either went missing that Monday, this was Sunday, so maybe on Monday."

Kitchener looked very weak and ill at that point. And no one believed that he had the strength to go far.

"I couldn't imagine him walking up that hill," says Shirley. "[But] he had an inner strength. Divine guidance, I don't know."

Lloyd Bogle believes that Kitchener knew the end was near and knew exactly what he was doing when he set off up the hill to Gully Lake on that Sunday or Monday. Lloyd recalls that Kitchener used to love an old British song "Keep Right on to the End of the Road," written and composed by William Dillon and Sir Harry Lauder, after Lauder's son was killed in World War I.

"He had told us many times that he was going to the end of the road," says Lloyd. "And we thought he was just talking about walking to the end of the old road that passed in front of his place up there in Gully Lake. That wasn't it; we just weren't listening to him, hearing what he was saying. He was telling us that he was really going to the end of the road, in both senses. That's what he did. He went to the end of the road – to die."

Corporal Don Gray of the RCMP detachment in Tatamagouche could not divulge the name of the person who called on the police to launch the official search that began on Wednesday, saying only that one of Kitchener's friends had called in to report him missing on that day. Hopes were not high that he would be found. The weather had been very bad, and to be out in it would have been an enormous challenge for anyone, especially an eighty-seven-year-old man who had been suffering with flu-like symptoms. There had been torrential rains on Monday, says Corporal Gray. Temperatures had then plummeted to minus twenty-five degrees Celsius on Tuesday, and when the search started they were dealing with a blizzard. The ground and air search lasted till Friday, when it was called off because of both bad weather and fears that if there were any chance Kitchener was still alive, the searchers were driving him deeper into the woods. Corporal Gray says it is likely Kitchener was dead even before the search had been called. All they did recover during the search was his green mountain bicycle, which had been abandoned part way up the hill to Gully Lake.

Lloyd Bogle and Shirley Sutherland Miller believe that the official police version is the right one – that there was no hope of finding Kitchener alive. Lloyd thinks the only reason they were not able to find his body in the December search is that they had misread his enigmatic comment about going to the end of the road, and limited the search to areas much closer to the cabin, underestimating his incredible strength and willpower, even at his advanced age and weakened as he was by illness.

As for suggestions that the search merely drove a sick man further into the woods, Lloyd says this is simply not possible. He is convinced that Kitchener died on the Sunday he left his cabin.

David Smith doesn't agree. He thinks that Kitchener took flight because he was afraid and running, fearing he would be forced out of his cabin and into a hospital or a home, and it was this fear that kept him running and hiding not just for weeks but for months after his initial disappearance.

"I saw him a couple of weeks before he went missing," he says. "He was cursing that day. In all the years I knew Willard he never cursed, not once. But that day he was using cursing words because he said there had been people out there bugging him, trying to get him to go into a home for the winter. That's what scared him. He thought they were coming to get him. The police wouldn't let any of us even help in the search, saying we had to stay away or go and register in Earltown before going near Gully Lake, while they went after him with helicopters that would only have driven him back into the woods further. If they had left him alone, I swear he would still be alive."

Dave Gunning, who along with John Meir had begun to write a song about Kitchener after their musical visit with him in April 2002, was so passionately moved by a search he believed was not warranted and certainly not wanted by the old recluse, that in December 2003 he and John sat down and completed their tribute to Kitchener, the song "Let Him Be."

The disappearance of and the search for Willard Kitchener MacDonald attracted a great deal of media attention, even making it onto the CBC national news and the Canadian Press wire, attesting to just how well-known he had become and how much his story, and the mystery of his past and his life, had sparked interest far and wide.

Cathy von Kintzel of *The Chronicle Herald* was one of the journalists who covered the story. She had met Kitchener only a couple of times before his disappearance; the first of these a few months before his cabin burned in 2003. She says he had been sitting on a rock, eating an orange and he offered her one. He had left quite an impression on her and she was particularly intrigued by his eyes. "They were deep, penetrating," she says. "He would stand back and look at you. We never look at the people we talk to, not the way he did."

A week after the search for Kitchener was called off, Cathy went in to his red cabin with Sherry Martell from the *Truro Daily News*. They were accompanied by Kitchener's friend "Clem" and his son, and the well-known Nova Scotian psychic and spiritual medium Alan Hatfield, from Pictou Landing, whom "Clem" had called in.

Cathy says there were many unnerving experiences that day. First were the orange peels on top of the snow near the cabin, despite the complete absence of footprints in the snow that would lend those peels a logical human explanation. She kept recalling how, the first time she had met Kitchener, he had offered her an orange.

Second were the voices and messages that Alan Hatfield "received." Alan says he heard several voices during his six hours in the woods that day, including that of someone called Howard who told him, "My boy's back that way," pointing up the road towards Gully Lake in the direction of the burned-out shack. Then Howard told him to go "four hundred paces from where the bike is located." Alan says he had no idea that Kitchener's father's name was Howard.

After receiving those messages, the searchers set out from the new cabin to try to get up the road to Gully Lake but they were unable to get very far because of deep snow and descending dusk.

The psychic used divining rods to pick up spiritual energy and a tape recorder with two microphones he set up near the front steps of Kitchener's cabin to capture "spirit voices." These he transformed to MP3 files – two-second bits of hiss and voices that I am not able to decipher, no matter how many times I listen to them. But with his experienced ear, Hatfield identifies one as Kitchener's voice saying, "I'm glad here." He contends that another captures an unknown male spirit voice saying, "Go . . . to the camper." And a third recording is of an unknown male spirit voice saying, "Get your coat on, Alan," followed by an unknown female spirit voice shouting, "Alan!"

In her article published on December 12, 2003, in *The Chronicle Herald*, Cathy von Kintzel quotes Alan Hatfield as saying his impression was that Kitchener "had passed over," and that he was "at peace."

Alan says he had gone in to visit Kitchener several times before his disappearance. To prepare for the December search, he says he used a dousing rod and a photograph of the missing man, and determined even before he went to the cabin that "Willard was already in spirit."

He notes that there was also a very tangible find that day. The journalists and psychic heard meowing under the red cabin. They removed the snow that had drifted around it and freed one of Kitchener's two cats that had been trapped underneath the cabin. Alan says the cat, grey with black streaks that he thinks Kitchener called "Tiger," was agitated and behaved very strangely, leaping onto their shoulders and moving ahead of them as if it were trying to lead them up the road towards Gully Lake. Cathy confirms that the cat's behaviour was not very characteristic of a feline as it led them up the hill, despite the deep snow.

Even if Alan Hatfield felt that Kitchener was "at peace," that is not what many of his friends were thinking. Some thought he was still alive and probably suffering, holed up in one of his remote camps to keep from being taken out for medical care or constantly on the move to avoid being found. Some worried that his fear of being found was so great that he wouldn't even make a fire to warm himself, despite the frigid temperatures.

Throughout the winter and spring of 2004, Ed Lorraine, former MLA for the area, says he would drop in to see his old friend Murphy Stonehouse in Earltown. "I would say to him, 'Kitchener can't still be alive, Murph.' And Murphy would answer, 'I haven't seen you for about six months but I'm not going around saying that you're dead.'"

Just as he had when he was living at Gully Lake, in his absence Willard Kitchener MacDonald was still keeping the rumour mill spinning. Stories abounded that he was alive and well, and not only that, he was alive and well and being cared for by friends in Loganville. And, typically, there were conflicting versions of just where he was and how he was living. Some said Kitchener was living in a cave or an underground hiding spot. Others said that people from Loganville were taking food into the woods for their friend. Others said that he was staying with the Smith family in Loganville.

In the spring of 2004, journalists Cathy von Kintzel from *The Chronicle Herald* and Sherry Martell from the *Truro Daily News* headed out to find out if there was any truth behind the rumours. They went to Loganville and knocked on doors, and after visiting with many of Kitchener's oldest and closest friends they left, convinced that no one in the area was sheltering him.

But even if Ruth Smith and her family did not know where he was, that didn't mean they believed for sure he was dead. When RCMP Corporal Gray visited her home, Ruth told him, "If Willard don't want to be found, you're not going to find him unless he's dead." When Corporal Gray replied that they would find him, Ruth quipped, "You didn't find him in the last sixty years. How do you expect you're going to find him now?'"

In the face of all the rumours, accusations and counter-accusations that were ricocheting about communities in northern Nova Scotia with different versions of what might have happened to Kitchener and why, in April 2004 once again psychic Alan Hatfield went in to see what he could find. This time there was no snow to prevent him from going all the way up to the site of the burned-out hut beside Gully Lake. Once again, there were many voices and once again, Alan says he was sure that Kitchener had "passed into spirit." But he was surprised to find at the site an unburned hardback copy of Farley Mowat's book about American primatologist Dian Fossey and her life – and death – with the gorillas in Rwanda's Virunga Mountains. This Alan took as significant in that he believed it related to his work in April 2001, when he had recorded the spiritual voice of Dian Fossey at the Calgary Zoo, in the gorillas' compound.

"We all were surprised that of all the books to find unscathed was indeed this one copy. Everything with spirit is relative and connected," he says.

It was this same book that David Smith placed on the top of the old stove the day he and Leroy Marshall sprinkled Kitchener's ashes at the site in July 2004.

In late June 2004, the RCMP and search and rescue teams headed up to Gully Lake, for a regular planned training exercise, which they decided to combine with a final search for Willard Kitchener MacDonald. Two men with dogs were brought in, the entire area around Gully Lake was divided into grids and marked with pink survey tape, and about one hundred searchers fanned out to scour the entire perimeter of the lake. They had not been able to do a thorough search of this area in December because of deep snow that, combined with the blowdown from Hurricane Juan, made the whole area almost impenetrable. They had also been leery of driving Kitchener further into the woods.

This time, it didn't take them long. At about two p.m. on June 27, 2004, they found the remains "of a deceased elderly man in a wooded area on the east side of Gully Lake." The spot where the body was found marked the end of an ATV trail that wound its way around the north side of the lake, passing just in front of the site of Kitchener's former hut. It was – quite literally – "at the end of the road." The RCMP said a birth certificate and other items found on the remains confirmed his identity.

Corporal Gray says an autopsy was performed and his death was due to exposure, hypothermia and his age, combined with illness. When he was found he was wearing a blue parka, grey wool pants, and heavy winter boots known as "Logans," the same clothing he was wearing when he was first reported missing more than six months earlier. Lloyd Bogle says he was also carrying the money order for nine hundred dollars.

In one of those remarkable twists of fate, the mother of Kitchener's unacknowledged son Leroy, Edna MacCallum (*née* Marshall), had died four days earlier and had been buried twenty-four hours before Kitchener's body was found on that Sunday.

David Smith doesn't believe the official version of Kitchener's disappearance and almost immediate death in December 2003. He believes very strongly that his old friend was alive long after he disappeared and he believes he "disappeared" because he was afraid of being taken against his will out of his cabin in the woods. After the search was called off, David says he went in searching for Kitchener each time it got a little warmer and there was a slight thaw. He says he walked many times over the exact spot where his body was found in June of 2004 and definitely saw his tracks in the snow in January. In his view, Kitchener probably succumbed to the elements during the massive blizzard of February 2004, a storm dubbed "White Juan" in Nova Scotia, coming just five months after Hurricane Juan struck the province. He thinks that Kitchener had gone up to another of his camps, near the "ear" of that topographical cat's head and that he was on his way back down out of the woods when he died.

David still has very powerful dreams about Kitchener, including one he spoke of at length in early October 2004, when he guided me up the back trail to Gully Lake to show me another of Kitchener's makeshift camps and also the abandoned bicycle propped against a tree, with the small Canadian flag on the handlebars. In the dream, he saw Kitchener cooking in a lean-to with three walls, in an old clearing where David used to go to get firewood near Juniper Meadow. It was very real and David intends to try to find more of Kitchener's hidden camps around Gully Lake.

Ruth Smith recalls the Sunday in June that she learned that her friend's remains had been found. "We were here in the kitchen," she says. "And a chickadee landed on the windowsill there; we never saw one there before. It was singing. We looked at each other and said that Willard must be sending us a message. I think it was. A half hour later the phone rang and it was Murphy, telling us that his [Kitchener's] remains had been found at the far end of Gully Lake."

"He always said he would come back as a bird," says David Smith. "A blue jay or a crow, because those birds are so beautiful. And he really liked to talk to the owls, especially after he had a couple of drinks in him. He would hoot with the owls."

Ruth recalls what he always said to her children at the end of his visits, when they wanted to know when he would come back, and how they would know he was coming. "He always said he would send us a message 'on the wing of a bird,'" says Ruth. And she is convinced he did that day his body was found.

Once again, the "Hermit of Gully Lake" made it onto newscasts and even editorial pages across the country – with articles announcing that his body had been found and recounting the legend of the shy old recluse, "the beloved member of the community" who had jumped a troop train. Close friends were worried that all the media attention would turn any funeral service they held into a media circus.

So Murphy Stonehouse, the Smith family and a few other people in Earltown organized a small service at the Community Church, keeping the list of those invited to a minimum, mostly people who had known him all their lives, people who called him "Willard" rather than Kitchener. Shirley Sutherland Miller, Lloyd Bogle, "Clem," and Jarvis and Lillie Stewart found out only that morning about the service, just in time to make their way to Earltown for the event.

On July 8, 2004 at two p.m., about a hundred people gathered in the Earltown Community Church for the service led by Pastor

Neil Stirling. Leroy carried a single rose for the hour-long memorial service. He sat alone in the pew reserved for immediate family. Lloyd Tattrie, a well-known fiddler in the Tatamagouche area, composed and performed a tune simply and aptly called "The Hermit of Gully Lake."

The Smiths and Murphy Stonehouse didn't quite succeed in keeping the press away, however, and the service even made it into *The Globe and Mail*, with an article by Shawna Richer headlined, "Poor old Willard? I don't think so," a direct quote from the eulogy delivered by Neil Stirling.

Neil says he spent two weeks interviewing everyone he could in the area about the man he calls Willard, trying to capture as much as he could of his character and his story, to write a meaningful service. He says it helps that he and his family had spent nineteen years living and working in Senegal in West Africa as Christian missionaries, because it offered them a perspective on hardship and how the lack of material comforts should not always be equated with poverty and misery. His speech painted a positive picture of the man and the life he had chosen to lead. Pastor Stirling has kindly granted me permission to reproduce some of his words here:

"During Willard's eighty-seven years I am sure the Shepherd made many special provisions for his needs of food, solitude, the chorus of birds, the beauty of sunrises, the beauty of sunsets, the blanket of fall colours that surrounded and covered his home, the wind in the trees, the crunch of leaves and snow under his feet (when that was the only sound).

"The warmth of the stove after being out in the cold getting kindling and firewood (our homes are always seventy degrees so we rarely have that experience) and the Shepherd looked after his healing those eighty-seven years. The doctors and hospitals of the country can't take credit; Willard would not go to their services.

"Willard saw the very first leaves turn reddish and orange, he was wrapped in its beauty throughout the entire season, he watched it reflected on the surface of Gully Lake, (maybe when geese and ducks were floating on that colour) and he felt those leaves fall upon himself, as the wind came through the forest, and he walked on a carpet more beautiful than anything you can buy in Halifax.

"I have sometimes heard the comment, 'Poor old Willard.' I'm not sure that in his personal life he wasn't richer than many of us. Possibly he was a great deal richer.

"Willard never had his computer crash, he never maxed out his Visa card, never got upset about lack of health care or insurance costs, never worried about what the Joneses had or didn't have, never owned an SUV, never got sued, never got pulled over for speeding or dangerous driving, and didn't even own a day minder or palm pilot that beeps forty-five minutes before the appointment that you *must* be at *on time*.

"Poor old Willard – not so sure about that one. Sometimes he came into town in the morning, sometimes in the afternoon – it just depended upon how the day went.

"I walked up the road to the Presbyterian Church this morning and back again. In Earltown, you are in the middle of one of the most beautiful green pastures of foliage and grassy fields you could ever imagine.

"Part of that blanket of green was the home of Willard Kitchener MacDonald. Some of us would agree that there is something restful in greens and blues.

"Those are the two colours that were all around the person of Willard most of his life.

"Those were the many shades of blue of Gully Lake and the greens of the forest that he loved so much.

"Poor old Willard – I don't think so.

"'He leadeth me beside the still waters.' Can you read those words and not think about Gully Lake this afternoon? You break out of the woods, and there is that rich deep blue looking back at you."

That service brought together a core of the people who knew and loved Willard Kitchener MacDonald the best, not all of whom wished to speak to the press (or to authors). They remained as protective of their friend after his death as they had been during his life.

After the funeral, Murphy Stonehouse reminded *The Globe and Mail* correspondent that there was nothing romantic about his life in the woods. "It was hardship, but he was a tough old nut," he told Shawna Richer. "He was a normal person to everyone here, but some people got into his business. He knew the kind of people he wasn't comfortable around. He was comfortable in your back yard, but not in the house."

Truro resident John Ansett, who had composed and performed a bluesy acoustic ballad in honour of Kitchener, told the *Truro Daily News*, "So many thoughts that go through my mind. I've got so many memories of him. Not only of enjoying his hospitality but of enjoying his concerts."

Many people were very touched by the service, such as Mable Murray of Tatamagouche, who wrote a letter to the *Truro Daily News* to say it had made her weep because of its wonderful simplicity, just what a "simple living man would want of his funeral." She was pleased that there were no florist bouquets, just simple bunches of field daises with moose-pea and a large bouquet of lupins with one single rose on his urn.

Not everyone looked back at Kitchener's life as one that – had he lived in a different time and under different circumstances – he would have chosen. Nor did they agree with those who romanticized it. Lloyd Bogle remains convinced that it was his decision to jump from the troop train that "dictated" the reclusive and difficult life to which he was condemned in the woods. He says it may have been a nice gesture to paint Kitchener's life as a rich one without many of the headaches and agonies faced by people in the work-a-day world, but adds dryly, "I bet no one would have changed places with him."

Chapter 15
Taking care of hermit business

The municipal and provincial governments wasted no time laying to rest the memory and the business related to Willard Kitchener MacDonald. On July 9, 2004, Harry Ashcroft, the Acting Director of the Land Services Branch of the Nova Scotia Department of Natural Resources, wrote to Wayne Faulkner of the Northern Regional Office Division of the Department of Environment and Labour, attaching a copy of the original letter of 1996 that laid out the terms on which Kitchener's cabin could be constructed on Crown land.

In his letter, written a day after the funeral, the Acting Director notes that "Mr. MacDonald has passed away" and quotes Clause Three of the letter that authorized the original construction.

"This authority cannot be transferred. This authority shall immediately terminate upon the demise or relocation of Mr. Willard Kitchener MacDonald and the land shall revert to the Department of Natural Resources. All structures shall, at that time, be removed within soxty days of the demise or relocation of Mr. MacDonald. Should, upon the demise of Mr. MacDonald, any heirs claim an interest in the structure they shall be advised of the conditions of removal."

And the letter goes on to say, "Given the foregoing, this letter will confirm that Letter of Authority No. 48, dated October 28, 1996, is terminated and of no force and effect. As the exact date of Mr. MacDonald's death is unclear, I request that your department have the structure removed from the subject Crown land within sixty days of your receipt of this letter. I am advised by our district staff that the structure appears to be in excellent condition and could easily be removed, in whole, without much effort or disturbance to the surrounding environment."

Not even two weeks later, the Municipality of Colchester County announced that the cabin would be auctioned off to the highest bidder, and called for tenders. Gary MacIsaac, Chief Administrative Officer in Truro, was quoted in an article by Harry Sullivan of the *Truro Daily News* as saying that the money held in trust for Willard Kitchener MacDonald, about $6,800 as of March 31, 2004, would be returned to the federal government after funeral expenses and any other outstanding bills owed by him had been paid. Sergeant Dave Darrah of the Truro RCMP says this complied with a codicil of the original agreement to grant Kitchener his old age pension, despite his refusal to sign for it.

Four bids came in for the Hermit's cabin, and the highest was for $4,250, from a man in the community of Economy. It was quite a bargain for a structure that cost more than twenty thousand dollars to build, money of course that came from Kitchener's old age pension trust fund.

The cabin was moved on the weekend of October 2, and the well was capped the following weekend. By then, it had been looted, the windows broken. Papers, books and the few belongings that Willard Kitchener MacDonald had left behind were strewn about the property like rubbish. Those were gathered up by government officials and sent to landfill.

The business of tracing any monies he might have had and locating "heirs" was passed on to the Public Trustee. None of the potential heirs – at least not Leroy Marshall nor Shirley Sutherland Miller – appears to have been informed of the removal of the structure in advance, which would have allowed them to express any "interest" in the structure. Leroy Marshall had offered publicly in the press and also directly to the RCMP to provide a DNA sample to prove he was Willard Kitchener MacDonald's son, but that was not followed up on before the cabin was removed. Shirley says the cabin was kept locked and that she was not able to get in after the funeral to remove the family mementos – photographs, tools and that clock – she had given to her cousin.

Times and attitudes seem to have changed considerably since the days when so many people in the municipal government had gone out of their way to find pension money for Kitchener and then to bend rules about the use to which Crown land could be put, by slicing red tape to ribbons and getting the red cabin built for him.

The provincial government had just completed a period of public consultation on whether Gully Lake should be designated a public wilderness area, and it seemed likely that would happen; Nova Scotia Premier John Hamm had made a promise to that effect in his election campaign the previous year. Given that Kitchener had been synonymous with Gully Lake, had made the name famous, it seemed logical (to me at least) that the Municipality of Colchester County might wish to erect some small memorial to the Hermit in what was bound to become an important hiking area and perhaps even a tourist attraction. Indeed, Leroy Marshall and David Smith had actually made a special trip up to the site to clear a good path that would allow a monument to be taken up the hill to Gully Lake, after they heard from people in Earltown that the County was planning to construct a memorial.

In October 2004, I asked Gary MacIsaac, if he, as Chief Administrative Officer of Colchester County, had given any thought to commemorating the life of Willard Kitchener MacDonald, who had after all become a living legend. I wanted to know if there had been any thought of naming a trail after him, putting up the rumoured memorial, something to note his passing and time spent in Gully Lake.

"No there is not," he replied.

"Do you think that would be a good idea?"

"I choose not to answer that question," he said, tersely.

In March 2005, the Government of Nova Scotia passed legislation to designate 3,810 hectares of Crown land around Gully Lake as a protected wilderness area. So, at least those who wish to visit the lake, pay homage to the man who lived next to it for four decades, and savour the quiet of the woodlands, will be able to do so. The area will remain the wilderness it was in Kitchener's time.

And a few weeks prior to that, Leroy Marshall, Kitchener's unacknowledged son, called me to say he had received a letter from the solicitor to the Public Trustee, stating that he would be invited to undergo a DNA test to establish his relationship with Willard Kitchener MacDonald. The reason? The old "impoverished" hermit whom so many had helped out over the years, not just with gifts of food and firewood and clothing but also to obtain for him a pension, died leaving a financial legacy, an undisclosed but allegedly substantial sum of money that he appears to have inherited from wealthy relatives, perhaps those in the United States or from his aunt Etta Silver.

Leroy says he is not interested in the money, but he does say the DNA test will clear up the matter of his parentage, so it can then be closed and laid to rest. It was not money he wanted from his parents, he says. It was acknowledgement and love.

Epilogue:
The legacy of the legend

"Finding out who he was, not where he was, was the hardest part of the search," says Sherry Martell, when she recalls the times she spent covering the disappearance of the "Hermit" for the *Truro Daily News* – the months afterwards with all the conflicting versions of what might have happened to him and the countless visits to the homes of those who knew him well.

Sherry had grown up in the area and visited the General Store in Earltown regularly with her grandfather to buy gumdrops. There she would inevitably hear people talking about the old hermit, asking how he was doing, wondering aloud if he was still alive. But in all those years she had never met the man and knew only the legend. After his disappearance, she says that even those who didn't particularly care for him and certainly didn't appreciate the way he had been turned into a folk hero didn't want to say anything untoward about him. He belonged to them and they respected his memory and his privacy.

In researching for this book, I have confronted many of the same challenges, puzzles and dilemmas.

Willard Kitchener MacDonald evoked many strong and conflicting emotions in those who knew him and even many who just knew of him. There are those who came to love the legend and the romantic portrait of the lone wise man suffering enormous hardship in the woods because he didn't wish to go to war and kill. There are those who respected his endurance and his strength, his talents and his imagination. There are those who just liked him because he came across as a soft-spoken and humble gentleman. There are those who pitied him for his loneliness, his delusions of grandeur about having once sung opera or gone without recognition for the things he claimed to have invented and created. There are those who idolized him, hung on his every word because he offered them such a novel and intriguing perspective on life and the world and because he was so different from the norm.

Some in the area are far less enamoured of him and the "legend" he became, noting that many people in Earltown lost family members who did not avoid military duty in World War II, and that many others worked their whole lives in the woods or on small farms eking out meagre livings, enduring physical hardship every bit as extreme as Kitchener's. They feel it wrong that he alone became a kind of "folk hero."

There had always been a certain distance between those who had known him since his youth and those who befriended him later on in life. Also, of course, there were still lingering differences among those who felt he had left his home willingly to die peacefully in the woods, and those who were convinced he had fled the warmth of his cabin in fear that well-meaning friends would force him into medical care or a home.

Just as there were people who knew him as Willard, those who knew him as Kitchener and the wider world that knew of him only as "The Hermit of Gully Lake," there were also divergent views on why he sought a solitary life in the woods. Some thought he chose the life he wanted; some believed he was more or less a prisoner of his own fears and a troubled past, sentenced by them to a life of isolation and hardship.

There is no doubt that Lloyd Bogle is right when he says it was not a life many would have chosen for themselves. Kitchener's hut was no utopian Walden and Gully Lake was no idyllic tamed pond, like the rustic hut beside the man-made pool that Henry David Thoreau called his hermitage for two and a half years in the mid-1800s. Thoreau wrote very compellingly about his experiences at Walden, how solitude offered him a new perspective on the busy and materialistic lives of people in a rapidly industrializing America, how possessions and beautiful homes, with large mortgages, were a burden rather than a blessing. Kitchener didn't seem to share Thoreau's interest in the mainstream society he had rejected.

In her recent comprehensive book, *A pelican in the wilderness: hermits, solitaries and recluses*, Isabel Colegate says that in the eighteenth and nineteenth centuries, romantics and philosophers liked to portray nature as a neat and loving place of peace and, through this, created the Transcendentalist movement. The French philosopher, Jean-Jacques Rousseau, best known for his depiction of the "noble savage," greatly influenced the growth of interest in a life lived close to nature, even though he reportedly did not much care for extended periods of solitude. Thoreau's experience at Walden was very much an extension of the movement that began in the eighteenth century, when, as Colegate writes, a "hermitage was seen as a rustic retreat for those moments when its proprietor or guests felt like indulging their melancholy or communing with nature, whose wilder aspects had recently become less terrible and more fashionable."

There was nothing romantic or fashionable about Kitchener's life or his hut. It was crude, dirty, and dark and it was set in a wild and rugged landscape in northern Nova Scotia, with wild and wicked winters. Kitchener was apparently neither familiar with, nor influenced by, any of the many hermit "movements" over the millennia and across all continents, when people sought solitude in caves and hovels or even in the middle of a desert for religious and philosophical reasons.

It's one of those wonderful human paradoxes that people who head off seeking solitude for whatever reasons – religious, spiritual, fear of the law (including military law) – wind up attracting large numbers of other people fascinated by their lives of solitude and the wisdom that many believe such an existence affords. Hermits orbit beyond the centripetal forces that constantly tug most people in towards the centre, demanding conformity. They are free to ignore many of the things that shape most of our lives: certain standards of hygiene; social rules, norms and niceties; family pressures and responsibilities; working hours; bank holidays; polite small talk and social discourse; civic duties and laws; paperwork, housework and filing. And yet ironically, after a time when word gets out about their lives of solitude, that solitude comes to an end. They start to exert their own centripetal force, attracting curiosity-seekers, sight-seers, journalists ever in need of a catchy and unusual story, people seeking to understand the recluse, people who seek to change them, who seek to care for and comfort them or be comforted. Some people come to admire or even worship them, believing they possess some great spiritual powers.

"We need hermits, cultural theory reminds us, because they give us a sense of respect for the person, just a person, whose mere presence reminds us that people are valuable even when they do nothing directly for the economy, the church, the environment, sports, the poor or world peace. We count them 'blessed' if they simply breathe," writes Hubert Morken. His 1997 essay "God Preserve the Hermits" appeared after the hermit in California, Theodore John Kaczynski, became infamous as the Unabomber and focused a lot of negative attention on those who live in huts and caves, as hermits or solitaries. Kaczynski, a Harvard graduate and mathematical genius, was a professor at the University of California Berkeley before quitting in 1969 and becoming a hermit after his application to immigrate to Canada was turned down. He sent bombs through the U.S. mail from 1978 to 1995, killing three and injuring more than twenty people, because of a dislike of technology and industrialized society.

Willard Kitchener MacDonald was certainly not a hermit who posed any danger to society. However, his decision to stay where he was when he had the means to move into more comfortable lodgings could be construed by some as a direct challenge or even an affront to those who felt no sane person could or would willingly shun the amenities on offer in this modern Canada of ours. The accoutrements of the "good life" that Kitchener shunned are the very things many of us spend our whole lives trying to obtain, our *raison d'être*.

There is even an unlikely but intriguing parallel between Kitchener's demise and the end of the far more famous, wealthy and powerful recluse in the United States – Howard Hughes, whose life was portrayed in the 2004 film *Aviator*. Hughes had amassed an enormous fortune in the oil, film, aviation and arms industries, meddled in politics and co-opted the CIA to hatch nefarious assassination plots, when he turned his back on the public life prescribed for the rich and famous. By 1970, not even his friend President Richard Nixon could contact him directly and he was never seen in public. Hughes died in an airplane crash, in a state of total self-neglect despite his vast land and business holdings and two hundred million dollars (U.S.) in cash; he left no will and when his jet crashed, he was said to be fleeing those who wanted to get him to Houston for medical care.

Hughes suffered from obsessive compulsive disorder, which had yet to be recognized as a condition that could be treated by therapy. In hindsight, some therapists believe this disorder may well have contributed to Hughes' decision to become a recluse. One can only speculate now as to whether Kitchener, with his particular likes, dislikes and eccentricities, might also have had any form of this condition.

Author Karen Armstrong in her autobiographical book, *The Spiral Staircase*, points out that the more solitary a person becomes, the more he or she is drawn into public life. "Crowds of people descended upon Saint Anthony, the fourth-century ascetic who lived in the deserts of Egypt, demanding his help and advice," she writes. "In our own day, the Trappist monk Thomas Merton had much the same experience."

Kitchener was not a masochistic ascetic and it's not obvious that he viewed his own lifestyle as particularly deprived. Nor is there any evidence that his flight into solitude at Gully Lake had anything to do with his faith. His privacy and self-imposed exile in the hills and woodlands around Earltown, Kemptown and Gully Lake were not a spiritual or political statement.

Nor was Kitchener's life as a hermit inspired by the vague but unrealistic desire that lurks in many of us born and bred in cities to escape from it all and return to nature. He was no stranger to the wilderness or to chronic poverty and hardship.

Willard Kitchener MacDonald was, as his friends say, "his own man." But like hermits the world over, he attracted many people of all walks of life, who had very divergent ideas about him and what he represented – if indeed he represented anything. Strange that a man who became a living legend because of his reclusive lifestyle in the deep woods of northern Nova Scotia should belong to everyone, but journalist Cathy von Kintzel thinks he did. At least the *legend* did, even if not everyone agreed on the meaning of the hermit legend or even on what kind of person was behind it.

A few viewed him as a rather lazy, unwashed reprobate. A few believe he was full of the devil. Others loved his old-fashioned good manners, his sense of humour and his humble demeanour. Some pitied him. Some believed he was almost saintly, anointed by forces ordinary people cannot feel or see, and they revered him. Some, those who knew him best perhaps, accepted him exactly as he was and didn't try to interpret or analyze him at all. As Isabel Colegate notes in her book on hermits around the world and through the ages, "There is a tendency to mythologize the solitary, whose story often turns out to be simpler than it first appeared. He is expected to provide a fable, or at very least, a symbol."

I am loathe to use this truism, but I feel I have to: Kitchener was who he was – and because no one really seems to know just who that was, everyone created their own version of the truth or legend. He left no one indifferent.

The man remains a mystery, an enigma – an unsolvable puzzle – and I believe he always will. I can think of no better way to end this book than with a refrain from the song, "Let Him Be," by Dave Gunning and John Meir:

> Let the woods grow tall around him
> Let the sun and rain surround him
> Let his music keep on sounding, let him be
>
> His world surrounds him
> The sun and rain's all around him
> His music keeps on sounding, let him be
> Just let him be

And with that, I now lay down this story of Willard Kitchener MacDonald. May he rest in the peace he so deserves, and his memory live on, free as the wind whispering through the trees in the woodlands of the protected wilderness around Gully Lake.

Acknowledgements

I cannot express my thanks emphatically or often enough to all the people who helped me with this project. Many went far beyond the onerous call of duty I imposed on them, opening up not just their minds to help me learn about Willard Kitchener MacDonald but also opening up their doors and their pantries and plying me with that legendary Nova Scotian hospitality – replete with tea and home cooking – as I plied them with endless questions and tried to separate the complex facts about the man who was their friend, acquaintance or relative, from the legend that was the Hermit of Gully Lake. Among them: the late Shirley Sutherland Miller who passed away just days before this book was printed; Leroy Marshall; Beth Henderson; Ruth Smith and her son David; Lloyd and Helen Bogle; Hector and Eleanor MacKenzie; Lillie and Jarvis Stewart; Viola Wall; Lloyd P. MacIntosh; Lillian Clarke; Robert Clark; Vonetta Mae Chouinard; Mildred Adamson; David Buckler and Corrine Trites; Alan Hatfield; Edie Bogle; Marilyn MacWah; Ed Lorraine; Merle Sullivan; Darryl Gamble; Harold Ferguson; Bobbie Watt; Bud Humphreys; and Miriam Travis.

My immense gratitude also to journalists Harry Sullivan, Cathy von Kintzel and Sherry Martell, who shared their wonderful "Willard stories" with me; to librarian Glenn Hamilton and Bernadette Martin at the Colchester East Hants Regional Library, Tatamagouche

Branch; to teacher, writer and Gully Lake runner Norris Whiston for sending me the story he wrote about Kitchener; to Pastor Neil Stirling for the detailed files he compiled and generously handed over to me; to Scott Campbell for permission to quote from his Bible story; to Paul Peterson of the Cambridge Military Library in Halifax for providing valuable articles and useful research advice; to Ron Wallis who offered historical tips about Pictou and research advice; to Graham McLeod of McLaren Funeral Home for his record-searching; to Tom and Doris Plestid who kept track of the news; to Corporal Don Gray and Sergeant David Darrah of the RCMP; and to the Nova Scotia Department of Environment and Labour in Truro for providing me with important documented history.

Thanks and congratulations too to all those who worked so hard to have Gully Lake designated as a protected wilderness area: the Ecology Action Centre, the groups that make up the Nova Scotia Public Lands Coalition – Pictou County Naturalists, Cobequid Salmon Association, Nova Scotia Salmon Association, the Nova Scotia Bird Society – and on the government side, Nova Scotia Premier John Hamm, Minister of Natural Resources Richard Hulbert, Minister of Environment and Labour Kerry Morash, Colchester North MLA Bill Langille, Pictou West MLA Charlie Parker, and the Municipalities of Pictou and Colchester Counties. Thanks also to Oliver Maas of the Department of Environment and Labour for his patience in responding to my questions about the proposed wilderness area around Gully Lake.

Enormous thanks to those who so kindly provided the photographs for this book: Dr. Gerry Farrell; the late Shirley Sutherland Miller and her daughter Susan Vincent, who found invaluable negatives and prints and copyedited this manuscript as she read it to her mother in hospital; Lloyd Bogle; Beth Henderson and the Pictou Historical Society; Hector MacKenzie; Harry Sullivan; Allan Sullivan; Mike Turner of the *Truro Daily News*, and Billy Sinclair. I also wish to express my gratitude to my father, Weston Baxter, for his meticulous work on the map of northern Nova Scotia. And my heartfelt thanks to Dave Gunning who allowed me to reproduce the lyrics to the song he and John Meir wrote for Kitchener, "Let Him Be," from his wonderful East Coast Music Award-winning CD, *Two-bit World*.

I have done my best to piece together the many disparate and sometimes conflicting pieces of the enormous and intricate puzzle that was Willard Kitchener MacDonald. The pieces were given to me by all those who agreed to be interviewed about him, but I take complete responsibility for any errors on these pages. The puzzle may always remain a few secret jigsaw pieces short of a whole picture.

As always, thanks go as well to my publisher, Lesley Choyce, to editor Julia Swan, to layout artist Peggy Amirault, to friends in Africa who followed the progress of the book from afar, and last but not least, to my family for their continued support and incredible patience.

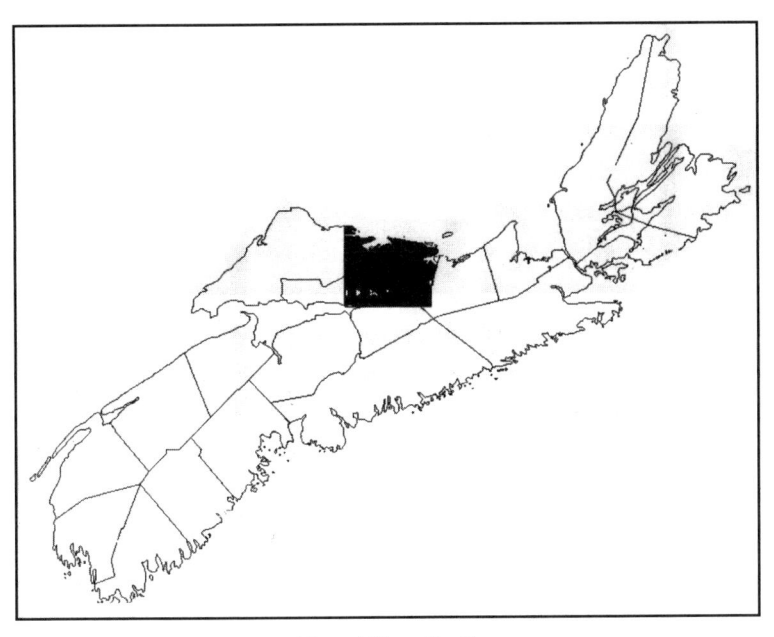

Map of Nova Scotia
Darkened area shows portions of Colchester and Pictou Counties
See maps on pages 156-157 for more detail of highlighted area.

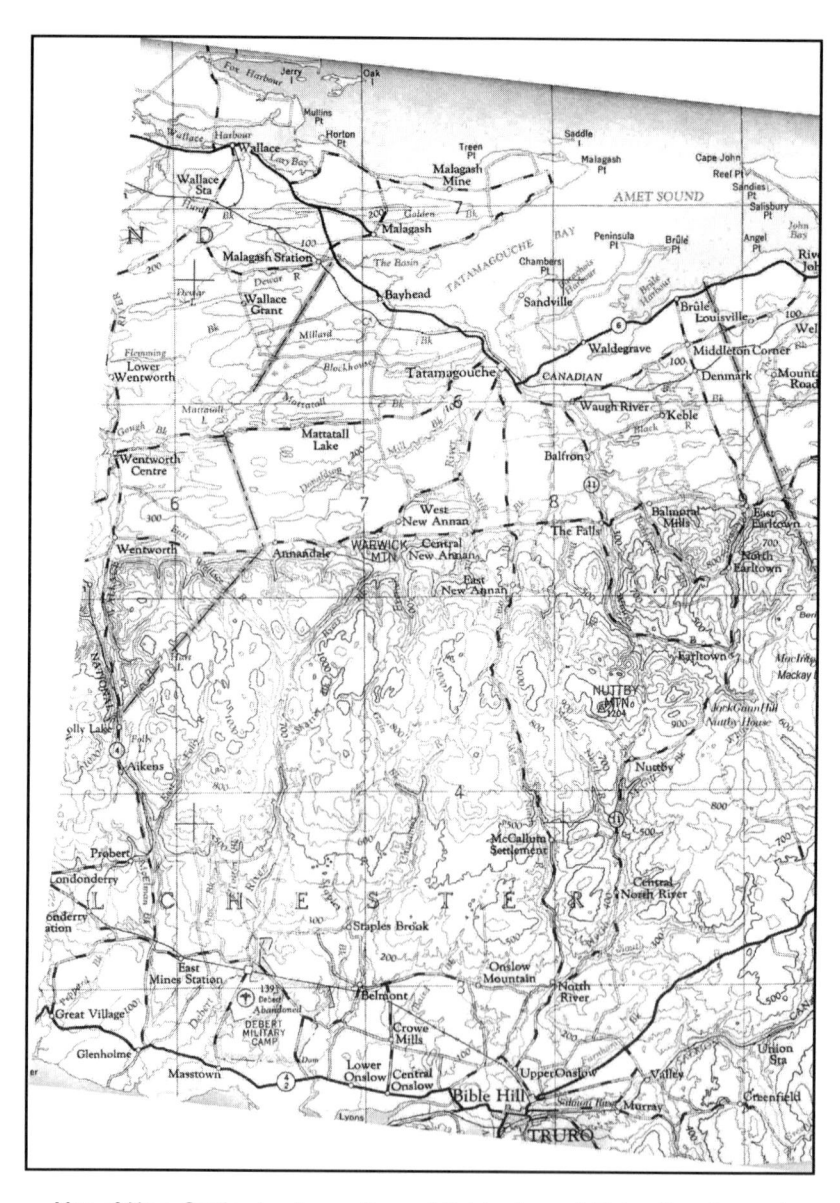

Map of Nova Scotia showing portions of Colchester and Pictou Counties and the area Willard Kitchener MacDonald called home. (Courtesy of Nova Scotia Department of Natural Resources)

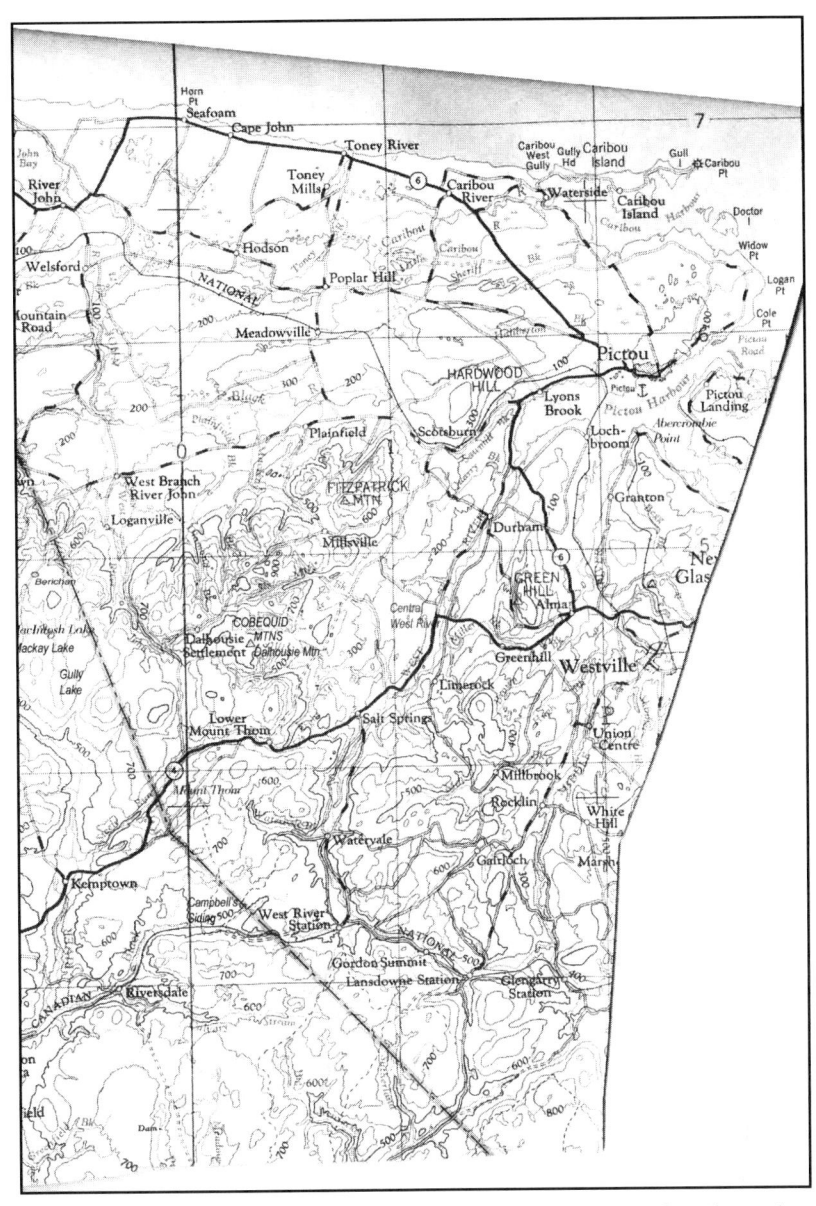

Map of Nova Scotia showing portions of Colchester and Pictou Counties and the area Willard Kitchener MacDonald called home. (Courtesy of Nova Scotia Department of Natural Resources)

Bibliography

Armstrong, Karen. 2004. *The Spiral Staircase: My Climb out of Darkness*. Toronto: Alfred A. Knopf. 2004. P 305.

Bonnell, Keith. 2004. "Friends remember shy recluse who spent 60 years hiding in NS woods." CP Atlantic Regional News. 8 July 2004. http://www.canadaeast.com/apps/pbcs.dll/article?AID=/20040708/CPA/37465025

Brown, Lesley, ed. *The New Shorter Oxford English Dictionary*. Oxford: Clarendon Press. 1995.

CBC Television News, 18 October, 2000; 7 February 1986; July 10, 1986.

Chouinard, Vonetta Mae (Stevens). *Vonetta's Memoirs of Beautiful Nova Scotia*. Nova Scotia: Vonetta Mae Chouinard. 2001.

Colegate, Isabel. *A pelican in the wilderness: hermits, solitaries and recluses*. London: HarperCollins. 2002. pp xii, 245, 250.

Dawson, Robert MacGregor. *Canada in World Affairs: Two Years of War 1939-1941*. Toronto: Oxford University Press. 1943. pp 47–49

Department of Environment and Labour, Province of Nova Scotia. June 2004. *Socio-Economic Analysis of Designating Wilderness Areas Within the Gully Lake and Eigg Mountain–James River Crown Parcels: Discussion Paper*.

Graham, Monica. A new name on paper: Neenah takes over reigns from Kimberly-Clark at Abercrombie mill. *The Chronicle Herald*. December 1, 2004: D1 and D7.

Graham, Monica. Son recalls life of hermit father. *The Chronicle Herald*, June 29, 2004: A2.

Graham, Monica and von Kintzel, Cathy. 2004. Sad end to hermit search. *The Chronicle Herald*, June 29, 2004: A1.

Howard Hughes. http://www.famoustexans.com/howardhughes/htm

Howard-Smith Captain Logan, Trusler, Thomas F. and Bryce, Viscount James. *Earl Kitchener and the Great War: The Heroic Career of One Whose Memory Will Live as Long as The British Empire*. Toronto: The John C. Winston Co. Limited. 1916. P 11.

Keep Right on to the End of the Road, written and composed by William Dillon and Harry Lauder, submitted by Betty Lauder Hamilton. www.sirharrylauder.com/lyrics/endroad.html

Keshen, Jeffrey A. *Saints, Sinners and Soldiers: Canada's Second World War*. Vancouver, BC: UBC Press. 2004. p 69.

Madsen, Chris. *Another Kind of Justice: Canadian Military Law from Confederation to Somalia*. Vancouver: UBC Press. 1999. pp 84–94.

Malloy, Jason and Sullivan, Harry. Gully Lake blaze destroys hermit's home, possessions. *Truro Daily News*. May 23, 2003: 1–2.

Martell, Sherry. Body believed to be "Hermit of Gully Lake" found Sunday. *Truro Daily News*, June 28, 2004:1.

Martell, Sherry. Psychic says spirit steering him towards Willard. *Truro Daily News*, December 12, 2003:1.

Martell, Sherry. Search continues for Earltown man. *Truro Daily News*, December 5, 2003:1.

Martell, Sherry. Search units scour woods for "hermit." *Truro Daily News*, December 4, 2003:1.

Morken, Hubert. God Preserve the Hermits. NeoPolitique, Robertson School of Government, Regent's University. 1997. http://www.neopolitique.org/Np2000/Pages/Commentary/Articles/hermit.html

Neary, Peter and Granatstein, J.L., eds. *The Veterans Charter and Post-World War II Canada*. Montreal: McGill-Queen's University Press. 1998. p 5

Nunn, Bruce. *More History with a Twist: True Stories from Mr. Nova Scotia Know-It-All*. Halifax, Nova Scotia: Nimbus Publishing Limited. 2001.

Proctor, Steve. Hermit spends time reading, snaring rabbits. December 28, 2000: *The Chronicle Herald*: http://www.canoe.ca/CNEWSFeatures0012/hermit_dec28-par.html

Richer, Shawna. 2004. "Poor old Willard? I don't think so." *The Globe and Mail*, July 9, 2004: A5

Smith, Amy. No logging allowed: two more wilderness areas protected. *The Chronicle Herald*. March 5, 2005: B1

Stacey, Colonel C.P. 1948. *The Canadian Army 1939–1945: An Official Historical Summary*. Ottawa: Authority of the Minister of National Defence. pp 232–235

Sullivan, Harry. Boyhood memories of the elusive "Hermit": Our paths have crossed on a few occasions – and Willard's path rarely crossed with anyone's. Reporter's Notebook, *Truro Daily News*, December 6, 2003: A1

Sullivan, Harry. Friends and family gather to honour the life of a "gentle man." *Truro Daily News*, 9 July 2004: 1

Sullivan, Harry. Gully Lake blaze destroys hermit's home, possessions. *Truro Daily News*, May 23, 2003: 1

Sullivan, Harry. Hermit's cabin to be sold, removed from Crown land. *Truro Daily News*, July 25, 2004: 5

The Hermit of Gully Lake. Editorial. *The Chronicle Herald*. July 11, 2004: A14

The Unabomber: major events in the life of Theodore Kaczynski. Associated Press 1998. http://www.unabombertrial/archive/1998/012298.06.html

Thoreau, Henry David. *Walden*. New York: Peebles Press International Inc.

Town of Pictou (history): http://www.townofpictou.com/index2.html

Von Kintzel, Cathy. Hermit's Gully Lake Cabin sells to the top bidder. *The Chronicle Herald*, August 1, 2004: A2

Von Kintzel, Cathy. Hermit "sharp as a tack right to the end," service hears. *The Chronicle Herald*, July 9, 2004: A1

Von Kintzel, Cathy. Hermit recalled for love of music. *The Chronicle Herald*, July 6, 2004: A1

Unity School of Christianity: http://www.religioustolerance.org/unity.htm